THE WISDOM OF 25 MEN OF INTEGRITY

TRANSPARENT LEADERS

DWIGHT L. JOHNSON

bookVillages

Men of Integrity: The Wisdom of Twenty-Five Transparent Leaders
© 2021 by Dwight L. Johnson

All rights reserved. No part of this publication may be reproduced in any form without written permission from Book Villages, P.O. Box 64526, Colorado Springs, CO 80962. www.bookvillages.com

ISBN: 978-1-94429-885-2

Cover and Interior Design by Scot McDonald
Cover image: istockphoto.com/ :BlackJack3D

Unless otherwise indicated, Scripture quotations are taken from the Holy Bible, New International Version®, NIV® Copyright ©1973, 1978, 1984, 2011 by Biblica, Inc.® Used by permission. All rights reserved worldwide.

Scripture quotations marked ESV are taken from The Holy Bible, English Standard Version. ESV® Text Edition: 2016. Copyright © 2001 by Crossway Bibles, a publishing ministry of Good News Publishers.

Scripture quotations marked ISV are taken from the International Standard Version (ISV) Copyright © 1995-2014 by ISV Foundation. ALL RIGHTS RESERVED INTERNATIONALLY. Used by permission of Davidson Press, LLC.

Scripture quotations marked KJV are from the King James Version (public domain)

Scripture quotations marked NASB are taken from the New American Standard Bible®, Copyright © 1960, 1971, 1977, 1995, 2020 by The Lockman Foundation. All rights reserved.

LCCN: 2021905326

Printed in the United States of America

1 2 3 4 5 6 7 8 Printing / Year 25 24 23 22 21

Dedication

This book is dedicated to my three sons: Dwight Jr., his wife, Trish, their three grown children—Shea, Emily, and Adam; Eric and his wife, Patsy, and their four grown children—Eden, Aiden, Cooper, and Cassie; and Stephen and his wife, Sara and their two daughters—Isabella and Tate. All three are born again believers and attended Promise Keepers conferences with me over the years.

Contents

A Note from the Author 7
Foreword by Tim LaHaye 9
Acknowledgments 11

01 Humility 12
KEN HARRISON

02 True Power and Security 22
CHUCK COLSON

03 Following the Real Leader 30
KEN BLANCHARD

04 Intimacy 38
RONALD HARRIS

05 Changing Your Course 46
ADOLPH COORS IV

06 Be Ready—in Season and Out 56
BENTLEY RAYBURN

07 Getting Past Superficiality 62
VINCE D'ACCHIOLI

08 Seeking God's Heart 70
BILL MCCARTNEY

09 The Character of the Leader 78
JAMES H. AMOS JR.

10 The Role of Challenges in Our Lives 84
HANK BROWN

11 The Significance of Spiritual Leadership 90
BILL ARMSTRONG

12 From Friend to Mentor 96
BOB SHANK

Contents

13 When God Changes a Heart 102
   GEORGE W. BUSH

14 Letting God Lead 110
   DAVE HENTSCHEL

15 The Unexpected Journey 118
   JERRY WHITE

16 Faith That Overcomes Doubt 126
   TOM LANDRY

17 Stuttering Well 134
   NEAL JEFFREY

18 The Abundant Life 140
   CAREY CASEY

19 Living for Others 146
   TOM OSBORNE

20 Turning from Darkness to Light 152
   ROSEY GRIER

21 The Truth Will Set You Free 160
   BILL KENNEDY

22 Second Chances 168
   CHRISTOPHER WILLIAMS

23 Be That Man 176
   TIM PHILIBOSIAN

24 Replacing Restlessness with Love 184
   JOSH MCDOWELL

25 Starting a New Legacy of Love 190
   DWIGHT L. JOHNSON

   Notes 199

A Note from the Author

When I decided to donate this book to the resurrection of Promise Keepers, which was the single greatest outreach ministry to men in the history of the world, and which was going to be done by Ken Harrison, a former member of the police department of Los Angeles as well as a millionaire real estate businessman, and Vance Day, a former lawyer and judge in the state of Oregon, I reviewed why I wrote the first of my three best-selling Transparent Leader books.

Tom Landry, perhaps one of the finest All-American University of Texas All-Pro New York Giant football players and greatest NFL Dallas Cowboy coaches said, "If you will put a book together about transparent leaders, I will write the foreword."

I sat down and started listing the men whose stories I would want to include. The list included Christian men whom I had gotten to know when I was on the worldwide boards of the Fellowship of Christian Athletes, International Board of Youth for Christ International out of Singapore, the West Coast Board of Young Life, and the West Coast Board of Prison Fellowship, and I realized that may well have been the reason I had been asked to serve on those boards.

Josh McDowell was the most sought-after speaker to teenage boys and girls in the world. Dave Hentchel's best friend's daughter led the grandson of Armand Hammer—the Russian Jew, head of Occidental Oil and Gas—to Christ. Tom Osborne, one of the finest college coaches, was my roommate at the second FCA conference at Estes Park. I spent part of three years with Rosey Grier, the All-American Penn State All-Pro New York Giants and Los Angeles Rams football player. Then there's Hank Brown, former president of the student body at the University of Colorado, former member of the US Congress and US Senate, president of the $1.6 billion foundation the Daniels fund, president of the University of Northern Colorado, and president of the University of Colorado, whose mom and my mom were in each other's weddings eighty-seven years ago. And Chuck Colson, the hatchet man for President Richard Nixon, who said, "Thank God for Watergate," which helped him commit his life to Christ, and thus founded Prison Fellowship.

These men and twenty others have allowed me to tell their stories in an effort to help men have the courage of their convictions to stand up to be counted for Christ, to be the men that God wants them and needs them to be as fathers, husbands, and friends. That is why I have donated this book to Promise Keepers, in hopes that the men and women who read this book will pray for the resurrection of Promise Keepers, make a tax-deductible donation to Promise Keepers, and pray that God will use this tremendous ministry to help us have a revival of this great United States of America.

Yours for the kingdom of God, Dwight L. Johnson

Foreword

There are two ways to look at the present condition of the world. One is to concentrate on the scandals in business, politics, sports, and entertainment and say, "What's the point in trying to live a Spirit-filled life? No one seems to care about character anymore."

Another way to look at the state of the world is to realize that there is more to the story than just ethical blunders. Instead of giving up, we can say, "Show me the people who are living honorably, faithful to God and their families during these trying times."

That's what you're holding in your hand right now. Put together by Dwight Johnson, this collection of stories tells of real leaders who have learned the eternal lessons of serving God in their work and their homes. These personal stories are shared by people who, just like you and me, sometimes wondered where God was in the midst of their experiences. Each story is different, but they also are similar in that they all deal with real-life issues and how God can use our circumstances to make himself known. All the men in this book faced some extraordinarily difficult circumstances. In all cases, God gave them an answer that was unique to them.

This book shows what living for Christ looks like in the present day. My prayer is that it will teach you how God can use your life to reveal his purpose in just as profound a way to the people you live and work with. Read this book, and apply its lessons to your own life to see how God is working out the answer specifically for you. Then pass it on to others who need it, and watch God answer their questions in a way that changes the world around them.

Tim LaHaye

Acknowledgments

It was a blessing to have my wife, Jeanette, help me with her good discernment as I put this book together. She had such a good, objective perspective on the different personalities and stories involved.

Karen Pickering and her team from Book Villages were such a huge help as we combined the first three books with the new personalities for this fourth book.

Finally, I am so thankful for the wonderful attitudes of all the men in this book and for their willingness to let me share their stories. I thank them for that trust and confidence and pray the book will be a true blessing to the kingdom of God.

I also wish to thank Steve and Brenda Bigori, Olin and Gloria Jones, Kevin and Sheri Stevenson, Tyler and Diane Miller, Frank and Ann Kocur, and Chuck and Joyce Newcomb for their financial assistance.

Ken Harrison

Dwight's Insight

When I met Ken Harrison, I was amazed at the diverse background he had for such a young man. The time he had with the LA Police Department, dealing with so many personalities, taught him how to interact with people in all kinds of circumstances.

He retired from the police department and started his own real estate business and learned how to deal with people buying and or selling property, and was extremely successful. Here again his ability to help people acquire property for different uses made it possible for him to understand a different side of the thinking process.

These two opportunities helped him realize how he could use his experience to answer God's call to participate in resurrecting Promise Keepers and assisting men to stand up to be the men that God wants and needs them to be.

Thank God for Ken Harrison and his willingness to take the lead for this incredible men's group, Promise Keepers.

—DLJ

Humility

Muhammad Ali became a legend long before ending his boxing career in 1981. Who of that older generation could forget him, and who of this present generation would want to? Ali was a global phenomenon. He made flamboyant claims, prophesying he'd win against the odds. Then he won, again and again, capturing the heavyweight championship three times.

Before his 1964 match against Sonny Liston, the 8-to-1 favorite who had knocked out the great Floyd Patterson in one round, Ali famously claimed, "I am the greatest. I said that even before I knew I was."[1]

Before his 1974 "Rumble in the Jungle" against the favored George Foreman, Ali claimed, "I'm gonna float like a butterfly and sting like a bee, George can't hit what his eyes can't see." Foreman later recalled that in the sixth round, Ali whispered in his ear, "That all you got, George?" Two rounds later, Foreman found himself on the floor.

Long before he changed his name to Ali, the young Cassius Clay fought hard in private so he could win in public. Someone asked how many sit-ups he did. He answered, "I only start counting when it starts hurting." Ali's quotes are favorites of motivational speakers, such as, "The fight is won or lost far away from witnesses, behind the lines, in the gym, out there on the road, long before I dance under those lights." What a champion.

Young fathers today may have seen Ali carry the torch to light the flame at the 1996 Atlanta Olympics. Perhaps the world's best-kept secret that night, Ali's sudden appearance on the soaring platform caused the arena, and the world, to gasp in shock. Then the crowd erupted as the former champion of the world, trembling with Parkinson's disease, held high that torch. People slapped high fives, cheered, and hoped against hope that Ali's shaking hands wouldn't drop the torch. Strangers in restaurants and bars and families at home watched TVs in awe, mouths agape, tears flowing, to see the beloved champion, diminished by disease, in a final, great Olympic appearance. Seniors flashed back to his 1960 Olympic gold medal, his famous bouts with Liston and Foreman, the brutal 1975 "Thrilla in Manilla" against Joe Frazier. Perhaps young fathers today will at some time hear Ali's name or see his image and turn to their children, as their fathers turned to them that night of the Olympics, and say, "That's one of the greatest champions of all time."

What endeared Muhammad Ali to the world? Wasn't he a loudmouth and a show-off? An arrogant bag of hot air? Why would factory workers, media pundits, farmers, and families all pause to watch Ali, catching their breath with tears streaming, as he held that torch to light that Olympic flame? Why didn't people hope the braggart would finally humiliate himself and drop the torch?

Many careers lend themselves to boasting and pride, and—let's face it—most men succumb to it. How do you admit your achievements without dropping into flat-out pride? A joke around airfields goes, "How do you know if there's a pilot at your party?" The answer is, "He'll tell you." Sorry, pilots, but I get it. In my life, I've been a Los Angeles police officer, a business owner, executive, and avid skier. Each lends itself to adopting a certain amount of swagger. How do we keep from having our status, our earnings, or our accomplishments affect us? How do we say, "I'm the greatest" at *anything* without being consumed by conceit?

Humility, it is said, is the willingness to remain anonymous. And it's more than that. Humility can be seen even in ultra-famous people. President Harry Truman lived by the maxim "It is amazing what you can accomplish if you do not care who gets the credit." Ronald Reagan went further, placing a plaque in the Oval Office that read, "There is no limit to the good a man can do or where he can go if he does not mind who gets the credit." These men obviously got the credit because their works were right out in the open. So, what is real humility?

Here are five attributes I believe contribute to humility and can be found in humble men, regardless of their status, fame, occupation, accomplishments, or lack thereof.

Humility Requires Strength

Men often equate humility with weakness. Moses could appear to have the most swagger of any character in the Old Testament, demanding that the most powerful man in the world "let my people go." (Exodus 5:1). And yet, Scripture records that Moses was more humble "than anyone else on the face of the earth" (Numbers 12:3) The fact is, Moses was humble *and* strong. His strength *originated* in his willingness to humble himself to obey God.

Jesus is often depicted as the "meek" Savior holding the little lamb, but would *you* want to argue with Him? Jesus' brilliant rejoinders to religious bigots are not just epic; they're *Scripture*. He was more than a genius—He was and is *God*. Christ's humility to come to earth and bear the burden of our sins required more strength than we will ever know. Jesus' life clearly showed that *it takes a strong man to be humble*.

All of us will be reviewed by the Lord when we die. What will I say when I stand before Him? Will I recount how much money I made, how many black diamonds I skied, or how many times I won at Scrabble? Of course not. The words we use that day are something worth considering long before we get there.

I've stood "in the dock" many times to answer for my actions. As an LAPD officer, I learned to choose my words carefully, to think about the person I was speaking to, and how my words were going to sound in a court of law. Instead of lambasting criminals who were hurting other people, I'd picture myself on the witness stand, defending what I said or did. In the same way, I picture myself standing before Jesus. How do I stack up? How does Jesus see me? What have I done with the gifts He's given me? When I think I'm okay, am I actually guilty of a false pride?

These questions are important. For a man to walk with the Lord and hear His voice requires humility, and humility requires strength. We have many great Christian speakers, pastors, and lay leaders, but sometimes when you get up close, you find they are not very humble. As a result, Christ's bride, the church, is smudged by human pride and led by human effort. Christian leaders even fall into scandal, just as secular leaders do. Often, they believe their own publicity. Or, perhaps unwittingly, they attract people who want the benefits of being near leadership and therefore say yes to everything the leader does or desires.

We need to be stronger and humbler than that.

Humility Requires Gratitude

As a young man, I went through officer candidate school. At the end, I secured a coveted contract to attend flight school. (If I had gone, you would have known when I was at your party, right?) Instead, I chose to follow my dad and uncle into the Los Angeles Police Department.

My police career started in the 77th Division of South-Central Los Angeles, better known as Watts or Compton. In this part of Los Angeles, 5 percent of its residents are extremely violent, but 95 percent are not. In our division's eight square miles, we averaged 180 murders a year. I averaged two felony arrests per day. I drew my gun six or seven times a day. Many times, I held people in my arms as they died. That leaves a mark on you.

It's humbling to see someone take a bullet while you didn't. It's humbling to see people lose their lives while yours was spared. It's humbling during a pandemic to see people lose loved ones while yours remain healthy. A big part of humility is recognizing that we're alive by the grace of God. Every breath we inhale is the breath God gives us, not just at birth, but every single day. Every morning we wake up is an opportunity to humble ourselves and thank God for another day. Humility requires gratitude.

Humility Requires Empathy

As an officer, I learned that no matter how well trained I was, there were people who knew more than me and people whose experiences could help me. Often, I had a lot to learn from people living on the streets in circumstances far different from my own. I saw up close how ethnically diverse we are as a nation. I had to learn to be sensitive to where people came from, what their background was, who their heroes were, how their values differed from mine. A variety of issues impact each of our lives, such as our faith, life experiences, and upbringing. I learned the importance of putting myself in another person's shoes. I had to consider, "How would I hear what I am saying if I were them?" It's called *empathy*.

When you're a police officer, you get a call, rush to the scene, and walk into chaos where you have to make split-second decisions. Then, months later, you are questioned by defense attorneys for every move you made in the two seconds you had to make a decision. You are judged and often condemned. It was humbling, but empathy helped. Putting myself in the shoes of the others involved in the case, I could answer without a negative attitude toward attorneys, judges, or anyone else.

Now, decades after my time on the force, I see tensions rising in our country everywhere—within companies, within educational institutions, within police departments. We could all benefit by gaining the ability to be *empathetic*.

And by the way, empathy also improves your marriage. Just think about the last argument you had with your spouse and ask, "How would I have responded to what I said if I were my spouse?" Many marriages could be saved through humility and empathy.

Humility Requires Admitting Need

A policeman in a big city sees death every day, then goes home to live among civilians. After years in the LAPD, I found myself struggling to talk with people who weren't police officers. Normal conversations seemed boring and stupid. I wanted to hide the toll the job was taking on me, but others saw it. One day my uncle, the LAPD officer, suggested I leave the force and start my own business. I had to humble myself to admit he was right.

Within a matter of years, I was as surprised as he probably was to find that I had built a small local company into one of the largest of its kind in the United States. My time in the police force had actually prepared me for business. When you're the guy in charge, you need to be able to work quickly on your feet, process information, and make big decisions that can have long-term effects. I found that I was efficient in my decision-making, and that made our company efficient in our work.

For two decades I enjoyed a commercial real estate career that went national. Then I sold the majority interest of that company to the second-largest commercial real estate company in the world. The deal required me to act as CEO over part of the company for the next six years. But one day, I got "the call." The chairman told me that an internal audit revealed that the business I'd sold them was almost bankrupt. He basically said, "Fix it."

I was devastated. What happened? What was I supposed to do? Once again, I had to humble myself. I was no longer the high-flying executive whose quick decisions could solve just about any problem. I was the low-crawling executive trying to hang on to my business but couldn't figure out how to get out of that dark hole. After six strenuous months of nonstop prayer with fear and trembling, God in His grace brought someone along whom I'd met years earlier. A government official secured a large contract with our company that turned us around. At my lowest ebb, I also called in a consultant who mentors CEOs around the world. He taught me so much that I am amazed I ever succeeded in business without him.

Admitting need is one of the most important things a man can do, and one of the hardest we'll ever do. Admitting need makes and keeps us humble. Admitting need makes and keeps us prayerful. Because of that, admitting need draws us closer to God, whose desire is to meet all our needs.

Humility Requires Willingness to Change

Christians see the Lord as someone who loves us no matter what, and it's true, He does . . . *but He loves us like a father*. A good father loves you, disciplines you, and rewards you. God continually takes us down a path to humility so we can hear His voice.

When I finally left business, I was exhausted. I thought I would go into ministry. Instead, I got comfortable with retirement. But after three years of outdoor sports and relaxation, I heard the Lord speak to my heart, *"Ken, I did not put you through everything so you can ski for the rest of your life."* I hesitated. Then I heard, *"Are you willing to be as ambitious for My kingdom as you were for your kingdom?"* I hesitated again. Then, *"Be careful of your answer—it's going to cost you your life."*

It wasn't easy to humble myself to make a big change at this point in my life. I was sick of being sued and stabbed in the back. I answered truthfully, "I feel like I've earned the right to take it easy for a while." Then I heard, *"That's okay, but you'll miss My full blessing."*

Oh! Wait—what? I wrestled with God for two hours. I saw myself being called to account on some future date only to learn that because I insisted on being comfortable, I missed all that God could have accomplished through me. Finally, I said, "Lord, I'll do whatever You want." He answered, *"I'll tell you when you're ready."* That was it. Huh? I wasn't even *ready* for the change He was bringing me? Ouch! I thought I'd graduated, but found myself back in kindergarten, learning new depths of humility.

That conversation with the Lord started a process of prayer, wrestling, and doors opening and closing as He humbled me further. Then Promise Keepers, the well-known organization ministering to Christian men, came my way. Today I serve as the chairman in a volunteer capacity, providing executive leadership and strategic direction while inspiring men to be bold and ambitious about their faith. And I also serve as the CEO of WaterStone, an organization that releases resources to support Christian humanitarian efforts worldwide.

Through this process of change, I discovered two things that come out of the humility to change: courage and generosity. And, if we're honest with ourselves, who would choose to live any other way?

What Are We Going to Do About It?

Looking over these five attributes, do you think Muhammad Ali could have had a measure of humility that people around the world could sense, if not name? As of a few years ago, George Foreman kept a photo in his office of his 1974 loss to Ali because it showed the danger of "not remaining humble."[2] Even after a caustic public relationship with Ali, Foreman maintains, "I love the guy."[3] What made youngsters like Mike Tyson "idolize" Ali? As a fourteen-year-old, Tyson promised to avenge Ali's 1980 loss to Larry Holmes. Tyson did exactly that, beating Holmes in 1988. But why? After all, Ali "the greatest" didn't really need defending.

What we know for certain is that Ali remained a champion not through his extravagant declarations, but through hard work. He failed financially, yet never shirked his responsibilities outside the ring, so he could be the best in the ring. He failed at marriage three times, and yet never shirked his responsibilities as a dad and became a beloved father of nine. He was a walking quote machine, a media minefield, yet he was resolute in his stand for racial equality and social justice.

How do we as men in the church stack up against Ali in terms of humility and conscience? Are we fighting the "good fight of faith" to be champions for our families? Or are we coasting, waiting for our kids to leave the house and for our wives to stop caring? Are we working out every day with prayer and Bible study? Or are we contenting ourselves with being spiritual weaklings? Are we humbling ourselves daily before God with gratitude and praise? Or are we succumbing to narcissism and conceit, as if our own efforts are quite good enough? Are we admitting need and joining small groups to overcome addictions to substances and pornography? Or are we hiding our faults while making our families pay the brunt of them? Are we willing to humble ourselves enough to change? Or are we entrenched in comfort zones we've created and don't really want to feel the Holy Spirit's nudge?

As I meet with and minister to men, I see a need for all of us to humble ourselves and repent. I see a need to accept our biblical identity as men, with Christ as our role model. As the world keeps shifting, I see the need for men to hold firmly what doesn't change—the Bible. Through Promise Keepers, I hope to play a role in calling men to this kind of championship Christianity. Because famous or not, rich or poor, old or young, humility is required of men. And certainly if we follow our Savior's example, humility is a sign of the man who loves Jesus Christ and desires above all else a relationship with Him.

02

Chuck Colson

Dwight's Insight

Many of us remember the Watergate scandal that resulted in the resignation of President Richard Nixon. One of the many names that Americans heard on the nightly news during that difficult period was that of presidential aide Charles Colson. For his role in the scandal, Chuck was sentenced to prison.

While admitting that his sentence was one of the lowest points in his life, Chuck also said it taught him the greatest lesson he ever learned: he had to first lose his life as a power broker to find his life as a follower of Jesus Christ.

As a result of his experience, Chuck launched Prison Fellowship Ministries in 1976 following his release. By 1979, Prison Fellowship groups had sprung up around the world and formed Prison Fellowship International, whose 116 indigenous ministries now make up the largest prison-ministry movement in the world.

Chuck passed away in 2012.

—DLJ

True Power and Security

I grew up during the Great Depression. I wanted security, wanted to find my meaning and purpose in life, and wanted to get a good education and a good job. I watched hungry people standing in breadlines and thought, *The most important thing would be if I could ever go to college.*

I won a scholarship to Brown University and graduated with honors. When I graduated, America was fighting the Korean War, so I joined the United States Marine Corps and was commissioned lieutenant. I remember the day I put the globe and anchor on my uniform, feeling great pride. I thought, *This is my meaning. My security is as a Marine Corps officer.*

When the war ended, I returned home, entered night school, and earned a law degree. I thought, *I'll find my meaning and purpose as an attorney.* I started a law firm, and it grew and became very successful.

I entered politics and became the youngest administrative assistant in the United States Senate. I thought, *I'll find my meaning and purpose in law and politics.*

The law firm continued growing and becoming more successful. I went up the ladder and, at age thirty-nine, was asked by the president of the United States to serve as his special counsel.

I started with an office way down the hall from President Nixon. Over time I moved closer and closer until I ended up in the office immediately next to him. I remember looking out over the manicured grounds of the White House and thinking, *My father was right when he said, "If you work hard, if you put your mind to something, if you really go for it, you can succeed and achieve the American dream."*

There I was, sitting in the office next to the president, walking in and out of his office every day of the week. It was one of the most powerful positions in the world. Limousines waited for me outside. Admirals and generals saluted me. It was everything a person could want. Curiously, though, despite all this success, I had the gnawing realization that I was as empty inside as ever.

After President Nixon was reelected in 1972, I decided that having served in the government for four years was enough. It was time to go back to my family and my law practice. And around this time, the Watergate scandal was just getting started.

Back to the Private Sector

One of the first things I did after leaving the White House was go back to Boston as general counsel to Raytheon, one of the largest corporations in America at the time. Its CEO, Tom Phillips, was a good friend, but I hadn't seen him during my four years in Washington.

On this particular day, I walked into his office, and I could tell right away that something was different about Tom. Fifteen minutes into the conversation, he began asking me about my health and how I was weathering what was becoming the Watergate controversy.

After answering, I said, "Tom, something's different about you. What's happened?"

He looked me square in the eye and said, "I have accepted Jesus Christ as my Savior and committed my life to him."

I had never heard anyone talk that way. I thought only little old ladies in tennis shoes who stood on street corners handing out tracts talked like that. I mean, here was a seasoned, practical businessman talking about Jesus Christ as if he were present. I had studied about Jesus when I went to Sunday school. I knew he was an ancient historical figure. But my friend was talking about him as if he knew Jesus personally. I nervously changed the subject.

Over the next few months, the Watergate scandal deepened. Patty and I would wake up and look out at our driveway to see it filled with camera crews. But every time I was with Tom Phillips, he still had that marked difference about him. He was kind and civil and seemed to care about me as a person.

One night I went to visit him. "Tom, you simply have to tell me what's happened to you. Why are you so different?" I asked. "What's this business about Jesus Christ?"

Tom's Story

Tom was the head of this huge corporation. He had a beautiful home, wonderful kids who attended the best schools, a Mercedes in the garage. He had everything a person could want, yet he felt empty. He told me about going outside and looking at the stars, all in perfect harmony and order, and as a scientist, he knew that there had to be something behind this perfect order. So he began a search for God.

He read about Eastern religions. He read philosophy. Finally, while in New York on business, Tom read in the newspaper that Billy Graham was preaching that night at Madison Square Garden. He had never heard Billy Graham, but he went to the arena, got a seat in the upper stands, and heard a sermon on who Jesus Christ really is.

Billy Graham preached that Jesus is not just an ancient historical figure but the Son of the living God, who rose from the dead and who lives today and who knocks on the doors of our lives and asks to come in. Tom made his way down through the crowd, stood before the stage, and gave his life to Christ.

Afterward, everything began to change. The hole inside began to fill up. His relationship with his family deepened. His attitude toward his business changed. As he told me this wonderful, moving story of his conversion, he read to me from an incredible book called *Mere Christianity* written by Oxford scholar C. S. Lewis, one of the intellectual giants of the twentieth century.

Tom read the chapter called "The Great Sin," which says pride is something we see in others but never in ourselves. A proud man walks through life looking down on other people and things, Lewis said. But when you're looking down, you don't see anything above yourself. You don't see God.[1] C. S. Lewis didn't know it when he wrote those words back in the 1940s, but he was writing them for Chuck Colson.

My Decision for Christ

Tom wanted to pray with me that night, but I didn't do it. I was too proud. I had prayed by rote in church, but nothing like what he was suggesting. But as I left Tom's home that evening, I borrowed his copy of *Mere Christianity*.

At that time, I had the reputation of being the toughest of the Nixon guys, the White House hatchet man, the ex-marine. But that evening, as I slid into the driver's seat, I found that I couldn't get the keys into the ignition. I was crying too hard.

I sat for a long time in my friend's driveway, thinking about my life, thinking about what he had told me about Jesus, and wanting more than anything else in the world to know God and be at peace with him. Finally, sitting alone in my car, utterly aware of my own powerlessness, I cried out something like "Take me, God. Take me the way I am!"

I was sure that the next morning I would feel embarrassed at what I had done. But I didn't. Instead, I felt a wonderful, wonderful sense of peace.

Shortly after that, I went to Washington, DC, and someone noticed me attending a prayer breakfast at the White House. Stories about my conversion went all over the world, and it was the frequent subject of network television coverage.

During the next few months, I realized that my newfound Christian faith was more on trial than anything I had done in Watergate. So one day I walked into the prosecutors' offices and told them that I couldn't plead guilty to what they were charging me with, but I *was* guilty of other things. I told them of something I *had* done and said that if they wanted to charge me, I would plead guilty. As a result, I received a one- to three-year sentence.

With Christ in Prison

It was in prison that I discovered the source of real power for change. The terrible thing about prison wasn't so much the physical deprivation. I had been in the US Marines. I could live in just about anything and get used to it. But I could never get used to seeing men lying on their bunks and staring into the emptiness with nothing to do, no place to go, nobody caring about them, their bodies atrophying, their souls corroding.

Seven of us formed a prayer group. Three were black; four were white: two dope dealers, a car thief, a stock swindler, the former special counsel to the president of the United States, and two others, on our knees at night, praying and studying our Bibles together. Other prisoners would come by, and we would talk to them. They asked what we were doing, and we told them what it meant to repent, to really know Jesus Christ, to turn their lives around, to be transformed. We would see these men give their lives to Christ, and the next day, their very stride was different—they walked without the prison shuffle. Their heads were up; they were transformed by the power of the living God.

People think the White House is where the power is. It's not. I saw in prison, where people were powerless, that the only power that really mattered was the kind that changes a human heart. And that can happen only through Jesus Christ, the Son of the living God.

After investing so much in striving to get to the top—to achieve success, power, money, fame—I found it all meaningless. In prison, with all those things gone, I found that we have identity, security, and meaning only when we are at peace with God and know him personally. All my years of looking for security—my education, my military appointment, my job, my position in government—ended up with my finding true security in God.

The Myths of the Four Horsemen

It's important for leaders in this culture to see how they can proclaim the gospel in all that they do and to understand why it's important that they do so. It's important to understand the future we're all trying to affect. Just as it was important for me to discover where true power is, I think it's necessary to see that power applied to our workplaces.

I believe that a struggle occurs today in regard to our future in general and our culture in particular. Each of us has an obligation to recognize and expose deceptions in the culture that are incompatible with our faith. We may very well find those deceptions where we are employed.

There are four great myths of our times, which I call the four horsemen of the present apocalypse. The first myth is the goodness of man. The first horseman rails against heaven with a presumptuous question: "Why do bad things happen to good people?" He multiplies evil by denying its existence. This myth deludes people into thinking that they're always victims and never villains, always deprived and never depraved. It dismisses responsibility as a teaching of a darker age.

It can excuse any crime, any bad behavior, because it can always blame something else, like the sickness of society or a sickness of the mind. But when guilt is dismissed as the illusion of narrow minds, then no one is finally accountable. The irony is that this myth should flourish in this modern age, with its gulags, death camps, and killing fields. As companies and as individuals, we must not diminish the importance of being accountable for our actions.

The second myth is the promise of the coming utopia. The second horseman arrives with sword and slaughter. This myth believes that human nature can be perfected by government. According to this myth, the new Jerusalem can be built using the tools of politics. Ruthless ideologies have moved swiftly from nation to nation on the strength of a promised utopia. They pledged to transform the world but could only stain it with blood. We have seen every utopian experiment fall, exhausted from the pace of its own brutality. Yet utopian temptations persist, even in the world's democracies. As leaders, we must put our faith in God, not in systems that continue to fail.

The third myth is the relativity of moral values. The third horseman sows chaos and confusion. This myth obscures the dividing line between good and evil, noble and base. It has created the great crisis of our day—a crisis in the realm of truth. When a society abandons its transcendent values, each individual's moral vision becomes purely personal. Society then becomes merely the sum of individual preferences, and since none is morally preferable, anything that can be dared is permitted.

The fourth modern myth is radical individualism. The fourth horseman brings excess and isolation. This myth dismisses the importance of family, church, and community. It denies the value of sacrifice and elevates individual rights and pleasures as the ultimate social value. But with no other principles to live by, men and women suffocate under their own expanding pleasures. Consumerism becomes empty, leaving society full of possessions but drained of ideals. This is what Václav Havel called "totalitarian consumerism."[2]

I have seen firsthand the kind of society these deadly myths create. I have visited more prisons than I can count in more nations than I can name. I have seen the crisis of modern times in human faces. They aren't just in prisons. They are in our companies, our political groups, and our churches.

True faith in God shows itself in humility. It shows itself in peace. It shows itself in service. It builds communities of character and compassion. We all see the culture we are part of, yet we don't have to be overwhelmed by it or ruled by it. Once we truly see the activity of God in society and in our lives, we are free to build his kingdom in our workplaces and homes. It is our task. It is our privilege.

Ken Blanchard

Dwight's Insight

I met Ken Blanchard at an executive outreach breakfast. The group was small, so we were able to have some fairly intimate discussions. When it came time for Ken to share, he told us about his spiritual journey.

It wasn't until the incredible success of his best-selling book The One Minute Manager, coauthored with Spencer Johnson, that he began to undergo a spiritual renewal. Over time the Lord became central in his life. He founded Lead like Jesus with longtime friend Phil Hodges.

Today Ken is chief spiritual officer of the Ken Blanchard Companies, which he founded in 1979 with his wife, Margie. The organization's focus is to unleash the power and potential of people and organizations around the world for the greater good.

—DLJ

Following the Real Leader

I am a follower of Jesus.

I am convinced that Jesus is a leadership model for all leaders, regardless of their faith.

Look at what he did. He hired twelve incompetent people who didn't have any of the skills relevant to the job ahead. He could have at least picked some decent preachers.

The first time I ever thought about Jesus as a leadership role model was shortly after *The One Minute Manager* was published in 1982. It became so popular so quickly that I was asked to appear on Robert Schuller's *Hour of Power* at the Crystal Cathedral. Reverend Schuller asked me, "Do you know who was the greatest One Minute Manager of all time? Jesus!"

"Really?" I asked.

"Sure," he answered. "Think about it. Jesus practiced the three secrets of the One Minute Manager—One Minute Goal Setting, One Minute Praisings, and One Minute Reprimands. After his goals were clear as to why he had come, he managed by wandering around from one little town to the next, catching people doing things right, and then praising or healing them. If they got off base, he wasn't afraid to redirect or reprimand people. He was a classic One Minute Manager."

This was the beginning of my examination of my own faith because the more I became exposed to followers of Jesus, the more I realized that Jesus had done everything I had ever taught or written about.

On God's Team

One of the first spiritual people to come into my life was Norman Vincent Peale, the positive-thinking pastor. He was eighty-six when I met him and still very active. I'll never forget what he said to me at one of our first meetings: "Blanchard, the Lord has always had you on his team—you just haven't suited up yet."

Of course, I resisted suiting up for a while because, as Dr. Peale would one day tell me, "The toughest test of self-esteem is to bow your head and turn your life over to the Lord. The human ego doesn't want to give up that kind of control." Given that reality, I didn't bite the bullet until about nine months later when we were having a major problem with our company.

A business executive we had made president was causing a lot of trouble. As I was driving to meet my wife, Margie, to talk about what we should do, I suddenly realized, *Blanchard, you are so stupid. Why are you trying to figure this all out by yourself?*

As I drove up the interstate, I simply prayed and turned my life over to the Lord. It became clear to me that I couldn't figure this or anything else out by myself. I needed his help. And as I prayed, peace came over me. My life has never been the same.

After I took the Lord into my life, I asked Dr. Peale, "Should I stop what I'm doing and go back to divinity school?"

He was quick to answer. "Absolutely not. You have a tremendous congregation out there, and we just don't have enough preachers in the field."

As a result, my personal mission became to be a loving teacher and example of simple truths that help me and others awaken to the presence of God in our lives. To me, that means teaching them how to be the servant-leader that Jesus wants them to be.

Learning to Be a Servant

In Matthew 20, Jesus took the disciples away to tell them that he was going to be arrested, falsely convicted, and crucified. Right after that, John and James's mother asked Jesus to let her sons sit beside him in heaven. They were hungry for power. When the other disciples heard the request, they became angry. Why? Probably because they wished they had thought of it first.

You would think that after spending three years with Jesus, they all would have known better. If I had been Jesus, I would have fired them all. But what did Jesus do? He saw this as a teaching opportunity. He had incredible patience.

> "You know that the rulers of the Gentiles lord it over them, and their high officials exercise authority over them. Not so with you. Instead, whoever wants to become great among you must be your servant, and whoever wants to be first must be your slave—just as the Son of Man did not come to be served, but to serve, and to give his life as a ransom for many" (vv. 25–28).

That doesn't sound to me as though Jesus was offering a plan B. He wanted his disciples to be clear that if they wanted to be first, they had to be last. If they wanted to lead, they needed to follow. He who is the humblest is the greatest.

Because of Jesus's mandate, I ask people, "Are you a servant-leader or a self-serving leader?" When I started asking that question, I was a little arrogant—as if to say, "I've got it, and you don't." Finally I realized that we all tend to be self-serving leaders to some degree. After all, the human heart is self-serving by nature.

There's nothing more self-serving than a baby. I have never heard of a baby coming home from the hospital saying, "How can I help around the house?" We all let our egos get in the way. To my way of thinking, ego stands for "edging God out" and putting self in the center of the universe. As a result, our journey from a self-serving heart to a servant heart is a never-ending one.

Why? Because we all fall short of perfection.

Scoring One Hundred

When I was seriously examining my faith, one of the things that bugged me about Christianity was the concept of original sin. Why do we have to start off bad? It didn't make any sense to me. I'm a humanist—why not believe in original potentiality?

Then I ran into Bob Buford, author of the fabulous book *Halftime*.

"Bob, why this original sin stuff?" I asked him.

"Do you think you're as good as God?" he asked.

"No, of course not. If there is a God, that's perfection."

"Okay," he said. "Let's give God a hundred and ax murderers a five. We'll give Mother Teresa a ninety-five—she was a pretty good person. You're not bad, Blanchard, because you're trying to help people, so let's give you a seventy-five."

I was able to follow him this far.

"The great thing about Christianity," he continued, "is that the Lord sent Jesus down to make up the difference between you and one hundred."

That made sense to me. I could more easily accept someone telling me that I'd fallen short of one hundred than someone calling me a sinner.

"Before you get too excited, though," said Buford, "let me tell you something you might not like as much. The ax murderer has the same shot at the ball as Mother Teresa. Grace is a gift; it depends on your acceptance of Jesus as your Savior, not your performance."

When I found out that Peter Drucker, the great management guru, was a believer, I asked him why he was a Christian.

He answered, "There is no better deal. Who else has the gift of grace?"

Remembering Our Priorities

What's the purpose of life? It's to enjoy a relationship with the Lord that operates every day out of love rather than pride. Some days turn out better than others, but the secret is to remember our priorities. When business leaders are controlled by ego, their identity is determined by whether they win or lose. They become their accomplishments—or their defeats. Self-serving leaders, led by their egos, care about gaining and maintaining power, status, and position.

If you give them necessary negative feedback, they kill the messenger. Why? Because they have to protect who they are, and who they are is their position. Servant-leaders, on the other hand, are really there to serve. If a better leader comes along, they're willing to step aside, willing to partner. They love feedback—even negative feedback—because it tells them how they can be better.

Sometimes when I mention this concept of servant leadership, people say, "I don't want to be a servant-leader because it's all about pleasing everyone. It's all about being liked."

Did Jesus please everyone? Was he liked by everyone? No. Whom did he really want to please? His Father. His Father had a vision and a mission. That's what Jesus came to do—to live out and communicate the vision and the mission of his Father.

The vision part of leadership asks, "Where are we going?" A lot of organizations don't know where they're supposed to be going or what business they're really in. But it's important to know where you're going, because leadership is about leading somebody somewhere. Even Alice learned that truth in Wonderland when she asked the Cheshire cat which way she should go.

"That depends a good deal on where you want to get to," he answered.

"I don't much care," she answered.

He said, "Then it doesn't matter which way you go."[1]

Likewise, if you don't know where you're going, your leadership doesn't matter.

Turning the Pyramid Upside Down

Years ago, I got to write a book with Don Shula, the legendary coach of the Miami Dolphins. He said that he became a great coach when he realized that he couldn't throw a pass, couldn't make a kick, couldn't make a tackle.

As a result, he felt his job was to help his players do those things well. Therefore, in a sense, Shula felt he worked for them.

He was always the first one on the field and the last to leave. He did whatever it took to prepare his players to be the best. Where did he get his strength and support? Shula said, "My day started best when I was on my knees, thanking God and asking for help."

For servant-leaders, the normal pyramid of how things work has to be turned upside down. How many of you have gone to your boss's house and the first thing he did was take off your shoes and socks and wash your feet? Yet that's what Jesus did for his "employees."

Why? Because it was one last chance for him to demonstrate to his disciples what they needed to know about servant leadership. Later, they would have ministries that thrust them into leadership roles. Now, before his departure, he was telling them, "Go out and share the good news that I have brought you. Go out and serve the mission. Go out and serve what we are trying to do."

We're in Sales, Not Management

Once, I asked Norman Vincent Peale whether he believed that Jesus is the way, the truth, and the life.

"Absolutely," he answered.

"So, what about the millions of people who never heard of him?" I asked. "And what about the millions of good people who heard about him and decided not to follow him?"

"I believe in a loving God," he said. "I'll bet he handles that in a loving way. I'm in sales, not management."

As Christians, we're all involved in sales. We're recruiting for the kingdom of God. And our mission isn't necessarily about results. It's more about what we can do to help. What can we do to support? What can we do to get people on the program?

That mission is opposed to the natural lure of earthly success, which is usually about money, recognition, and power. That's what most people push and shove for. Nothing is bad about any of those things in and of themselves. What's bad is when you judge who you are by them.

The opposite of earthly success is spiritual significance. Instead of money, the issue is generosity. What's the opposite of recognition and achievement? Service. What's the opposite of power and status? Loving relationships.

We all fall short of one hundred. But by helping the people God sends our way, we help us all.

04

Ronald Harris

Dwight's Insight

Ron Harris and I have been friends for many years. We met soon after Ron became a Christian in 1971.

Ron was senior vice president and cashier of the First National Bank of Denver during the 1970s and had many opportunities to share his faith with other people in the business community. He subsequently served as executive director of a Christian missionary organization, then as a senior executive of business enterprises in the Denver area. He retired in 1997 but stays active in the ministry of helping others.

—DLJ

Intimacy

Most business books and articles I've read talk about the importance of good relationships with customers, investors, and employees. Managers are instructed on how they should act around their people. Some experts recommend wandering around the workplace and being accessible; others say to socialize with employees, while yet others suggest maintaining distance from the workers.

All this sometimes-contradictory advice is important at some level because it addresses the importance of relationships, and good relationships are crucial to success in business. But there's another relationship that's often ignored by businessmen, yet it's the most significant one of all—and that's a relationship with Jesus Christ. And second only to that spiritual relationship with God is another that is usually passed over by books and articles on business success. In fact, it's the relationship that gets the least amount of attention from businesspeople but has the highest priority in God's eyes—and that's the relationship a married businessman has with his wife.

How a man relates to his wife will have a direct effect on his relationship with Christ as well as his business life.

Form over Substance

I got married when I was twenty-two, still at the age when I thought I knew it all. No one needed to teach me anything. We had children early in marriage, and I set out to do what I thought I was supposed to do in the world. My understanding was that life was about success, title, money, and power. I was seeking form over substance. All my emphasis was on how I could get ahead.

When my wife announced she was leaving me, I said, "We have three children; we have a nice house; we have two cars; we have a dog; I'm vice president of a bank. What are you talking about?"

She said, "There's nothing going on between us. You've got your golf game and your job. But we don't have a relationship."

I didn't have a clue as to what she was talking about. I thought we had a great relationship. As I look back, I know that what she was really telling me was that we didn't have an emotionally intimate relationship. But even if she had said those words then, I wouldn't have understood her. Her decision filled me with shock and despair.

My idea of a relationship was on the physical plane. As long as we had a great sexual relationship, we had a great relationship, right?

Listening with One Ear

Part of leaving your father and mother to marry someone means that you're leaving behind that old relationship to form a new one with another person. You're connecting in new ways with your spouse. It also means loving that person as much as you love yourself. It means being willing to die for that person. I'm not just talking about physically dying for her, as in taking a bullet for her. There's no heroism in that. I'm talking about dying to who you are and being willing to become the person she needs you to be.

I am convicted by the fact that I cannot tell you that I have always known my wife's heart. I have not been that man of understanding who could draw her out and make her feel free enough to share all that was on her heart. I wasn't mature enough or enough of a real man to hear and understand her. I have also not been the kind of man who could fully share my heart with her. I kept my heart guarded for many years, yet my wife had been saying, "Let's share our hearts with each other." I didn't know what she was talking about.

I am very results oriented. So, when my wife would begin to tell me about something, I was thinking about the solution to the topic she was describing. But that's not what she wanted or needed at all. I was impatient and selfish, and those were some of the things God convicted me about when I became a Christian.

"Guess What Happened to Me?"

As you can imagine, things were pretty tense in our marriage after she told me she wanted out. I got a lot of sympathy from my friends, which didn't really help. But I was in despair. I didn't want my marriage to end. I had three kids under the age of ten, and I loved my family to the extent that I could understand the meaning of love.

In my desperation, I sought out a former boss. Lee once had invited me to attend a Bible study with him. He also invited some other guys from the office. He wanted to meet one morning a week at a local restaurant to read and talk about the Bible. I didn't want to do it, but I did it because he was the boss.

It was a terrifying experience because if you attended, you had to lead occasionally. The person who led the discussion also had to lead the prayer before breakfast, so I took my Episcopal prayer book, held it low under the table, and read from it, pretending it was really me praying. I did this for a year, just to get ahead.

Now my marriage was falling apart, and I was a mess. I sought out Lee, and he shared his testimony again. He told about the problems he had had in his relationship with his wife. She had become a Christian and had grown more interested in a relationship with her Christian friends than with him, and this caused him great concern.

One night a bunch of her church friends were at the house, and she was in the kitchen with the women, while he was in the living room with the men. One of the guys said, "Lee, you look kind of down in the dumps." He said, "Yeah, I guess I need you guys to pray for me." They prayed for him, and he committed his life to Christ.

That brief account was his testimony. I wanted to hear it again, so he told it to me in twenty-five words or less, and then he prayed. He didn't pray specifically for me and my salvation, but he prayed.

I drove home in my little Mustang convertible, and as I was passing the Denver Country Club, I said, "Jesus, if you're who Lee says you are in his life, then I need you in my life. I need your forgiveness. I need to confess to you that my whole life has been going in the opposite direction from where you want me to go."

Immediately I felt Jesus's presence in that car. It was real. Here I was, a guy whose personal life was in shambles, and suddenly God was present in the car, giving me assurance for the future and forgiveness for the past, and I knew it.

One of the first things he convicted me of was my selfishness, that my priority had been my career, my title, making money, what others thought of me, my golf handicap. I loved my wife and my kids, but God convicted me that they were more objects for my pleasure than anything else. So I drove home and said to my wife, Maribeth, "Guess what happened to me?"

I told her everything, but she thought I was trying to convince her that things were going to be good. However, for the first time in my life, I wanted Christ to be the center of our family. At dinner that night, I shared it all with the kids. They were pretty young, and they said, "Yeah, whatever," and wandered off. But Maribeth and I talked until late at night. And God blessed that.

A few weeks later, Lee dropped a brochure on my desk, announcing that a man named Larry Christenson, author of *The Christian Family*, was coming to a church in Denver. I had been a Christian only for a few weeks and felt that I had a huge deficit in my life that needed to be filled, so I wanted to be wherever Christian people were. I went to the service and was surrounded by the praising and worshipping—something I had never experienced before. At the end of the service, I didn't want to leave.

Larry Christenson spoke from James 5:14–15: "Is anyone among you sick? Let them call the elders of the church to pray over them and anoint them with oil in the name of the Lord. And the prayer offered in faith will make the sick person well; the Lord will raise them up." That sounded good to me. My daughter, Andy, suffered from epileptic seizures. They were severe, and she took a lot of medication.

I talked with Larry about her, and he said that I could bring her over and that he would pray for her. I went home, told Andy about it, and asked, "Do you believe Jesus heals people?"

She said, "Yes."

I nearly fainted. My wife had taken her to Roman Catholic catechism, and Andy told me she had heard that Jesus healed the lepers.

By gosh, she's right, I thought. On Monday, during her lunch hour, I picked up my seven-year-old girl from school. Larry talked with her briefly about Jesus being a light in her life, anointed her with oil, and prayed for her. Then we left.

I took her back to school, I went back to work, she quit taking her pills, and God healed her of the seizures. My wife couldn't believe it. I could believe it because I didn't know any better. I was a brand-new customer. I never had any struggle or confusion over it.

But my wife said, "What's the deal here? What are you doing to our children? You become this whacked-out Christian guy, and now you're doing all this wild stuff to our children."

But even while she was hammering me about these things, God gave me the grace not to be defensive. She began to see that this truly was a change in my life. And Andy said to her, "Mom, I don't need to take the pills anymore. Jesus healed me."

Maribeth also saw the books I had been leaving around the house, so she read some of them, and by the end of the year, she committed her life to Christ. Our marriage survived.

Two Connected Relationships

Why is it important to connect at a heart level? Because, by doing so, we take a giant step toward connecting with the Lord. Trying to connect on an intimate level with the Lord while not connecting on an intimate level with our wives is almost impossible. The two relationships are connected. Listening to our wives share their hearts, growing in that relationship, propels us into a more intimate relationship with the Lord. And if men think their wives are hateful, angry, critical, or just plain hard to please, it may be that they're frustrated because they have yet to experience an intimate relationship with men who are honestly striving to be the image of Christ.

Intimacy with our wives leads to intimacy with God. But we lack training in the area of intimacy. We have a lot of pride that gets in the way. Our upbringing gets in the way. But this is what God desires of us. He tells us in Ephesians 5 that our relationship with him is the model for our relationships in our homes (vv. 25–33).

In Matthew 7:23, Jesus said, "I never knew you. Away from me, you evildoers!" I've thought about that statement a lot, and I don't like the sound of it. In effect, Jesus was saying that he didn't have a heart-to-heart relationship with those people. They didn't connect at that deep level. Jesus was saying, "You did things in my name, but I never knew you."

His words are very similar to what my wife told me at the end of ten years of marriage. Her telling me she was leaving was another version of "I never knew you." We had a house, kids, and a sexual relationship, but we didn't know each other. We didn't connect at that deep, heart-sharing level.

God saved our marriage. He saved Maribeth and me. And by drawing us into a closer relationship with each other, he drew us into a closer relationship with him. If he can do it for us, he can do it for you.

05

Adolph Coors IV

Dwight's Insight

I met Adolph Coors IV when my wife, Betsy, joined the Junior League. Husbands were often invited to events sponsored by the group, and it was at one of these functions that I was introduced to Ad.

Ad is a living example that having the courage of your convictions and pursuing the plan that God has for your life are more important than an earthly heritage.

He has spent years traveling around the country, sharing how God's grace saved not only his life but also his marriage and his calling as a man of God. Ad and his wife, BJ, have two grown sons and make their home in Colorado.

—DLJ

Changing Your Course

My name, Adolph Coors, is very familiar to a lot of people. Some have said that the Coors family is the embodiment of the American dream. I don't know whether that's accurate, but we did have grand hopes and aspirations, as every family has. The Adolph Coors Company in Golden, Colorado, grew into one of the largest breweries in the world.

The founder, my great-grandfather Adolph Herman Joseph Coors, lost both of his parents when he was fifteen. He was trained as a brewer in his native Germany, and in 1868, at the age of twenty-one, he came to America to avoid the German draft. He arrived unable to speak English and with only a few cents in his pocket. He made his way out west and eventually found work as the foreman of a brewery in Naperville, Illinois. By 1872, he had made his way farther west and landed in Denver.

He and a business partner bought an abandoned tannery in Golden, about twenty miles west of Denver, where they could start their brewery. In 1880, he achieved his dream. He bought out his partner and adopted the philosophy "Never give up, and success is attained."

My great-grandfather devoted his entire life to his brewery. His foresight was such that when Prohibition came to Colorado in 1916, he had already established a pottery company and a bottling operation to make up the lost income. He also began to manufacture malted milk, and soon the Coors Company was the third-largest producer of this product in the United States.

Years later, on the morning of June 5, 1929, tragedy struck our family. Adolph Coors Sr. fell to his death from a sixth-story window of a downtown hotel in Virginia Beach, Virginia. The official story was that he had become despondent over problems at the brewery, and after staying up all night with friends, he fell to his death. Was it suicide? Quite likely. My great-grandfather learned the hard way that wealth, prestige, and power aren't the ultimate source of gratification.

By the time I arrived on the scene, the Coors family had regained some stability. The first fourteen years of my life were like a beautiful Norman Rockwell painting. I was part of a loving, close-knit family with two older sisters, one younger brother, and two fantastic parents. We did everything together.

I remember wanting to grow up to be just like my dad. Adolph Coors III was a remarkable man. As a successful businessman, he was chairman of the Adolph Coors Company. But he was also a private pilot, multi-talented athlete, cattle rancher, and pioneer in the development of skiing in Colorado.

But with all his great accomplishments, the only thing that stands out in my mind about my dad is that, as busy as he was, he always had time to spend with us. He loved us, and he didn't mind showing it.

However, I regret to say that there was one missing element to this Rockwell painting. Almost every Sunday morning, as a young boy, I found myself in church with my sisters, but I don't remember my mom or dad ever coming with us. They were a vital but missing element to our Sunday mornings.

Life Does Not Shout; It Just Runs Out

When I was thirteen, my father grew tired of living in the city and moved our family to our ranch in the foothills west of Denver. He had designed and built our beautiful home, which to me was like the perfect American dream home.

But, as is true for all families, life brings many changes. Some are sudden; some are gradual. Some are welcome; some bring pain. One tragic day in 1960, the fabric of this wonderful family was violently torn apart. All that was the Coors name, all our legacy, couldn't protect us.

February 9 was bitterly cold, typical for Colorado at that time of year. As usual, my father was up early, ate breakfast alone, and left the house before I saw him. Through the falling snow, he made his way from our ranch toward the brewery. As he drove down the same road he had traveled countless times before, he noticed a yellow 1951 Mercury parked on a small bridge. Wanting to help, he stopped and approached the driver of the car. But the man didn't need assistance. He had been waiting for my father. It was a day the man had been planning for two years.

The two men fought. As my father ran back toward his car, the attacker, an escaped convict from California, repeatedly shot my father in the back. With my dad's body stuffed in the trunk, the man sped off. A passing milkman found the only clues as to what might have happened two hours later: my father's baseball cap and glasses—and blood on the bridge railing. Dad's car, with the motor still running, was a few yards away.

For seven long months after my father's disappearance, we didn't know whether he was alive or dead. As the FBI investigated, my family held out faint hope that Dad would return to his loving family. But it didn't work out that way. Dad's remains were found near a dump site forty miles away. Life does not shout; it just runs out—sooner than we think.

When our family got the news that Dad wasn't coming back, I saw my radiantly beautiful mom change before my very eyes. Hatred for the man who brutally murdered her husband began to consume her. Then she turned to alcohol in an attempt to fill the tremendous void and hurt in her heart. She drank to excess, and we kids were powerless to stop her.

I enrolled at a small college in Georgia but was emotionally unable to handle the responsibility of being on my own. I majored in fraternity and sorority and minored in academics. I lasted one year.

The Age of the Half-Read Page

I spent the next three years in the United States Marine Corps. With the name Adolph Coors, it didn't take me long to discover that if I were going to survive, I had to quickly become very tough. I was consumed with proving that I was a rougher and tougher marine than anyone else, and I was committed to not failing in this assignment.

A lot of people bet that I wouldn't make it, but my life reflected the saying "Pride is like a man's shirt—it's the first thing on and the last thing off." I masked my tremendous insecurity with the macho marine image. The saying "He who falls in love with himself will have no rivals" applied to me.

During this time, I refused to think about my own death. Was I ready? Was my passport in order? I didn't care. Even after my older sister, a proud mother of a new baby boy, died of cancer, I continued in my denial of my own life running out.

After the Marine Corps, I married my high school sweetheart, BJ. Unfortunately, we spent our first several years together buying things we didn't need to impress people we didn't like. Our lives were similar to how much of America lives. We would leap out of bed early in the morning, off and running. We would turn on the radio or TV, brush our teeth, get the coffee going, shower, get dressed, and go to the office. Late in the day, we would come home, have dinner, watch some more TV, go to bed, and so on, day after day, week after week, year after year.

Henry David Thoreau said, "The mass of men lead lives of quiet desperation."[1] That pretty accurately described the lives my wife and I were leading, as well as the lives of most of the people we knew.

The Emptiness of Material Wealth

Most of us fail to recognize that the bait of wealth hides the hook of addiction and eventual slavery to our possessions. John Rockefeller once said, "I have made many millions, but they have brought me no happiness."[2] Henry Ford Sr. reportedly once told a friend, "I was happier when I was doing a mechanic's job." Why were these successful men able to admit that there was something missing in their lives? God created us with "batteries not included." He has placed a spiritual vacuum in the heart of every human being that can't be filled by any created thing. It must be filled by him, or we remain empty.

In the early days of our marriage, I buried myself in materialism, hoping that something would finally give my life some meaning and purpose. I thought owning a mountain home would most certainly be the answer, so I purchased a beautiful lakefront home in the mountains. Every weekend, always surrounded by friends, we would spend two frantic days trying to be happy.

I continued trying to carry the burden of the Coors name the only way I knew how: by striving first for success, then for more and more money. I went to the University of Denver Daniels College of Business and set a personal goal of becoming a millionaire by the time I was thirty. I had five years to accomplish my goal.

A nagging question kept visiting me, though. *Adolph, why do you feel so empty?* No answer came, so I continued my quest for financial gain. I began to invest heavily in Colorado real estate and in commodity markets in Chicago. Unfortunately, an unexpected change in the national economy caused huge losses in real estate and commodities.

My goal shifted when I joined the family business, the Adolph Coors Company. This time, my goal was to become the youngest president in its history. I wanted to follow in the footsteps of my dad, my grandfather, and my great-grandfather. Frantically I climbed the corporate ladder, so caught up with what the world defines as success that, in the process, I was destroying those closest to me, my wife and baby son.

In all this gaining, I was losing. Someone has said that success is getting what you want but happiness is wanting what you get. I was successful but not happy.

Searching for Meaning and Purpose

Early one October morning, while returning home from work, I suffered a near-fatal car accident. While recovering, I began to take a hard look at my life. I was facing the embarrassment of financial ruin and living in a marriage that was heading for divorce.

I continued to search for the one thing that would lighten my burden and give my life some real meaning and purpose. A lot of people run to drugs, booze, an affair, an experience, in order to find peace, joy, purpose, and meaning. I was one of them.

I asked all the questions. *Who am I really? Why am I here?* I was experiencing that spiritual vacuum that God has placed in each of us, a vacuum that longs to be filled. My life was in total shambles. I despaired over ever amounting to anything.

Eventually the injuries from the accident healed and I returned to work. But shortly thereafter, my life at the Coors Company took a dramatic turn. I began working for our vice president of administration, who had been hired by my father many years earlier. He had known me most of my life.

One evening BJ invited this man, Lowell, and his wife, Vera, for dinner. Over that meal, they shared the truth of Jesus Christ with us. Through them we learned the truth of John 3:16, that God so loved us—his creation—that he gave his one and only Son so that anyone who believed in him would be saved and have eternal life. God took on flesh and blood and came to live with us in the person of Jesus Christ.

A few days later, BJ invited Jesus Christ into her life. The void she had been experiencing was immediately filled. When she made that decision, I saw a dramatic change in her. Deep down, I knew that she had found the one thing that I desperately needed. But I still wasn't ready to give up the struggle. Pride is the only disease that makes everyone sick except the one who has it.

It wasn't long after this that my wife and I agreed to a separation. During those painful weeks away from my family, I began to listen for the first time to what God was so clearly saying to me. For years I had shut my mind to him. I had been running so hard from God. But I couldn't continue that way. I was, at long last, coming to the end of myself. When you finally realize you're nobody special, you quit worrying about making a comeback. And apart from God, I was a nobody.

I began reading a book Lowell gave me called *Do Yourself a Favor: Love Your Wife* by H. Page Williams. I learned the importance of applying God's priorities to my life. Mine obviously weren't working. The most important priority was a personal, ongoing relationship with my heavenly Father. Second, I needed to love my wife with the selfless *agape* love that can come only from God. Feelings come and go, and true love can't be based on something so transitory. It has to be based on commitment. Third, I needed to develop a close relationship with my son. That wouldn't come unless I was willing to devote quality time to that relationship. Last, the book showed me that I needed to cultivate true friends. True friends are like diamonds, precious but rare; false friends are like autumn leaves, found everywhere.

Changing Course

One afternoon, while still separated from my family, I went to hear a man speak in downtown Denver. As I sat in the auditorium, surrounded by hundreds of people, his words deeply penetrated my heart. He quoted Acts 4:12: "Salvation is found in no one else, for there is no other name under heaven given to mankind by which we must be saved."

Later that day, by an act of my will, I opened my heart and life to Jesus Christ. I said a simple prayer, and as I did, Jesus filled the void that I had tried to fill for nearly thirty years. The truth of God's unconditional love began to flood my entire being. I had never experienced that kind of love. Suddenly the one thing I had been looking for was finally mine.

The things that had been so important to me no longer were. For the first time, my marriage to BJ and my relationship with my son took their proper place in my list of priorities. My ship was changing course. BJ and I agreed to make our marriage work. We discovered that a good marriage is a union of two forgivers. I was beginning to learn that not only is love finding the right person; it's also being the right person.

It was important for me to realize that this new relationship with Christ wasn't just a belief in a religion. Religion won't do anyone any good. It's nothing more than a feeble attempt to cross a barrier that separates a person from God. This simply won't work, because the Bible makes it clear that man's righteousness is inadequate for his salvation.

God doesn't love us because of who we are or what we can do. That's religion. God loves us because of who he is and what he has already done. This isn't a religion; it's a relationship.

BJ and I shared our good news with my mother just before she left for a short vacation. Mom was interested as we told her how she could invite Jesus into her life. After a brief but meaningful conversation with both of us, she departed and promised to call us when she returned. But three days later, Mom suffered a major stroke. A few hours later, she died. Life does not shout; it just runs out—sooner than we think.

Forgiving the Unforgivable

Even though I had accepted Christ, one area of life still gave me tremendous trouble. I had developed intense hatred for the man who murdered my dad. The FBI had arrested him in Vancouver, British Columbia, and brought him back to Colorado, where he was sentenced to life in prison.

But hatred is like acid that can't be poured without spilling on the raw heart that held it. I can say from experience that hate hurts the hater far more than the person hated.

Jesus Christ began to impress on me the need to forgive the man who had killed my dad. I tried on countless occasions, but I wasn't able to do it. If forgiveness was going to come at all, it was going to have to come from a source higher than me.

Jesus loved me enough to go to the cross and die for me. Romans 5:8 says, "God demonstrates his own love for us in this: While we were still sinners, Christ died for us." As I began to comprehend this beautiful truth, it became painfully obvious that I had no right to hate another human being—not even the man who murdered my dad. Forgiving would involve a decision on my part. But I knew I wasn't capable of that kind of forgiveness. By searching in God's Word, though, I found my answer: "I can do all this through him who gives me strength" (Phil. 4:13).

Finally I went to see my dad's killer. Three separate times he refused to see me. So I wrote him a note, asking for his forgiveness for the hatred that I had in my heart for him for so many years. I also said that I forgave him for the pain and suffering he had caused my family and me.

As I was obedient to what Jesus Christ asked me to do through his Word, he did what I could never have done for myself. He removed the hatred that had burned in my heart for so long. In its place he put love that could come only from him. The process of true and complete forgiveness can begin only when Jesus enters your heart—not before.

The message that was beamed to me through God's Word and through his servants was that I needed to change course or I would crash. I am so grateful that I got the message before it was too late.

Christians are like lighthouse keepers who direct other people to pay attention to the light. We're the ones sending signals to those in the world who believe they can manage on their own. The world needs more people like Lowell and Vera who can shine a message of hope to people who are headed for destruction.

Will you be in the lighthouse for Jesus?

06

Bentley Rayburn

Dwight's Insight

My best friend and last business partner in Colorado, Will Perkins, introduced me to an outstanding man and strong leader, Bentley Rayburn. I have been so impressed with Bentley's ability to pick up on a number of interests in the community and how he and his wife, Debbi, do such a good job of staying involved with their family.

Bentley retired as a decorated major general in the US Air Force. Throughout his life, he has put first things first—his relationships with Jesus Christ, Debbi, and his children. What a blessing he is to those of us who have had the privilege of getting to know him and the wonderful contribution he makes wherever he is.

—DLJ

Be Ready–in Season and Out

My grandfather was a Presbyterian pastor who traveled as an evangelist all over Kansas, Oklahoma, and the Panhandle of Texas. My dad's oldest brother was also a Presbyterian pastor and the founder of the youth ministry Young Life. I have two older sisters who married Presbyterian preachers and an older brother who—you guessed it—is a Presbyterian preacher. And me? I am a trained killer.

Before you get the wrong idea, I should clarify that I am a major general in the US Air Force.

After serving in Korea, Dad took a position as the founding president of Covenant College in Pasadena, California, where I was born. After only one year, the college moved to a campus in St. Louis, Missouri, where Dad became president of the new Covenant Theological Seminary. I sat at our dinner table with many of the great men and women of the evangelical church. J. Oliver Buswell was a professor in the seminary along with R. Laird Harris and Elmer Smick. Francis Schaeffer and his wife, Edith, were routine guests at our home, as were Os Guinness, Joel Belz, David Peterson, and so many others.

In my senior year of high school, I applied and was accepted by the United States Air Force Academy (USAFA). My father didn't have any objections to my going to the academy, though he counseled me that I would be wise to attend Covenant College for a year to get a good foundation in Bible and theology. Of course, when you are eighteen, a year is a long, long time, and I was eager to get on with school in Colorado. Now, in hindsight, I see the wisdom of his advice and how better prepared I would have been for the challenges that came my way.

The USAFA

People often ask why I went to the academy as opposed to going into the "family business," the pastorate. I'm not sure of all the reasons, but I do know that watching my father put on his uniform and go off to his Army Reserve training was a real source of pride. People often talked of his heroics in the Korean War—though he would have been the last to claim to be a hero—and that had a profound effect on me as well.

I was fortunate as a junior to be selected as a squadron first sergeant, the top junior in one of the squadrons. In my case, Twenty-Seventh Cadet Squadron, the Thunderbirds. The cadet wing has forty cadet squadrons organized into four groups of ten. During my time at the academy, cadets were given different leadership opportunities during each of the three periods of the academic year—fall, winter, and spring.

During the winter of my junior year, I was selected to be on the third-group staff, and then in the spring, I was selected to be the wing sergeant major—the highest-ranking cadet in my class. The summertime at the academy is full of training routines, leadership opportunities, and usually three weeks of vacation. I knew my life was going to be busy when I became a senior, so I elected not to take leave but to take the flight-screening course during my first summer training period so I wouldn't have to deal with it during the academic year. It was good that I did, as I was selected to be the cadet commander for the first period of basic cadet training (BCT) for the class of 1978 and then also served in the second three-week period of BCT before the 1974–75 academic year started.

Being given so much responsibility while still a cadet was fundamental to my eventual air force career. They say that the academy is, among other things, a leadership laboratory. And in my case, that was certainly the truth. I worked daily with senior officers and with my peers, not only to carry out the directives of the commandant of cadets and his staff but also to lead the cadet wing.

Torrejón Air Base

When we got on the airplane and sat down, the older man next to me asked where I was going. I told him I was a new F-4 pilot being assigned to the 401st Tactical Fighter Wing at Torrejón Air Base in Spain. Much to my surprise, the man replied that he was going to be my boss. John Winkler was being assigned to the 401st as the deputy commander for operations. Needless to say, I was kind of on pins and needles for the rest of the seven-hour flight to Madrid.

We arrived in Spain and were met by a few of the folks from the 613th Tactical Fighter Squadron. A friend who had been on the Air Force Academy soccer team and was also in Spain graciously let my wife, Debbi, and me use his small car to find an apartment.

Spain was a real adjustment for Debbi. She had grown up in a Christian home and gone to a Christian college. Spain and the life of a jet fighter squadron were completely out of her comfort zone, especially since my squadron deployed a lot. Being newly married with her husband gone was not easy. But the Lord provided some lifelong friends, and Debbi tried to minister to many of the other wives.

As I look back on our time in Spain, I am struck by how the Lord changed the hearts of so many people over the years. In fact, I suppose I doubted that even he could change the hearts of some of those profane, rough-around-the-edges fighter pilots. But he did. Many of those hardened individuals came to know the Lord, which is a testament to the fact that his ways are not our ways and that he can call even the wildest folks—those who seem unreachable—to him.

Being Ready

In leadership, you need to be ready. You never know when you are going to be called on to do something, big or small. But as a leader, you must be ready because unexpected challenges will always be part of a leader's life.

At the Pentagon, I was assigned to the secretary of the air force staff group. We supported the secretary in his position as the senior civilian leader of the air force. It was a very interesting year, as shortly after I arrived was the national election of 1980. While in DC, I took up the effort to earn a master's degree. It was common knowledge that to be promoted in the air force, you really need an advanced degree. I found a program at Georgetown University focusing on national security issues that was being taught right in the Pentagon. The problem was that the program took two years, and I was supposed to be working there only one year. How could I make this work? Even doubling up and taking twice the course load, I couldn't get it done in a year.

Providentially, one of the officers in my fighter squadron in Spain was now working fighter pilot assignments for the air force from his base in Texas. When I explained that I needed to stay in Washington through the fall of 1981, he simply moved my training date in the F-16 to January 1982 with a report date that would allow me to finish my studies at Georgetown. I checked out in the F-16 at Hill Air Force Base in Utah. I was originally programmed to be assigned to one of the operational squadrons at Hill after my transition course, but because I had already been an instructor pilot in the F-4, they decided to have me check out as an IP in the F-16. By doing so, I was able to meet the requirements for the F-16 fighter weapons instructor course taught at Nellis at the earliest opportunity.

Leadership Lessons

Over the years, I have learned a lot about leadership—sometimes the hard way. But there really is nothing new under the sun. You can learn more about leadership by reading the book of Nehemiah (an account of events that happened more than two thousand years ago) than you can by reading management books written by the latest leadership guru.

In a nutshell, I have learned that leaders need to be approachable. People in your organization must know that they can talk to you, if need be. Yes, there is a chain of command, but if subordinates feel that they are going to get their heads bitten off if they bring bad news, then the obvious will happen—you won't get the important information you need.

Leaders face a host of challenges. The three biggest that I see continually are the need for technical competence, the need to make good decisions, and the need to set and keep the right priorities. Technical competence is, in short, knowing your job and doing it well. As a young fighter pilot, I was responsible for the safe operation of my aircraft, which meant knowing the flight manual and all the associated information. As I rose in rank and responsibility, I still had to know how to employ my aircraft, but now I needed to know how to do more things well. Though you don't necessarily have to be the best at every task your company or enterprise does, to be effective and to have the respect of the people who work for you, you must be known as one who knows your job.

Leaders make decisions, most of which are easy and straightforward. Some decisions, though, can be much harder—and many of these hard decisions, I have found, involve people. But even in these cases, you usually know the right thing to do. It just takes courage to do it.

The few situations when you just don't know what to do usually, again, revolve around people. I suggest that leaders develop a small coterie of close associates—best if they are not in your organization—to call for advice. And of course, leaders need to be willing to take that same phone call from someone else on occasion and give the best advice possible. In the end, a leader must do the right thing. Sometimes it takes a great deal of courage when one group is pushing in one direction and you know that the right thing to do is to go in the other direction—but that is the responsibility of the leader.

Another tough thing, not only for leaders but for everybody in our modern world, is to set and keep the right priorities. All the technology we have at our fingertips can be a wonderful advantage. But we all know that our cell phones and computers can also be terrible time wasters. Many things in our modern lives scream for our attention and time. Good leaders must set the proper priorities, not only for their organizations but for themselves as well. Some of the most important things in life don't necessarily show up on our calendars. Our children, for example, are one of our most important priorities, yet we often haven't spent the proper amount of time with them.

Ask yourself what your legacy as a leader will be. The biggest influence on your long-term impact may well be your successor. Have a succession plan on the books. It also is important not to change things just to make your mark. Change for change's sake is not worth it. Make changes because they will benefit the organization, not because they will benefit your personal agenda.

And no matter what field you are a leader in, consider what your spiritual legacy will be. Will you be known as someone who prays for wisdom or does his own thing? Be humble and approachable and willing to serve others. That is the kind of leader I want to follow.

07

Vince D'Acchioli

Dwight's Insight

A good friend recommended Vince D'Acchioli as an excellent resource and motivational speaker. Over the years, I have come to know Vince both as a personal friend and as an effective leader in the Christian community.

   Vince is the founder of On Target Ministries, an organization dedicated to helping people discover and live out God's plan for their lives. He is also the author of Wired to Work! Vince and his wife, Cindy, have two daughters and reside in Monument, Colorado.

—DLJ

Getting Past Superficiality

As I travel throughout the United States and Canada, speaking to groups, I often ask the audience, "How many of you are satisfied with our modern culture? How many think we are headed in the right direction?" The response is minimal. The next question I ask is, "If you had to lay the blame for our condition anywhere, where would you place it?" A lot of people respond by pointing to the government, political leaders, educational institutions, and the media.

While all of these are powerful and oftentimes negative influences, I believe that the real blame for our condition lies squarely at the foot of the church of Jesus Christ. God intended for his followers to act as beacons, shedding light in a world of darkness. We must begin to take that responsibility seriously.

Suppose you were to ask a feminist, "Tell me the first thing that comes to mind when I say *evangelical Christian man*." What do you think her response might be? I don't know what she would say, but I can tell you what she *wouldn't* say. She wouldn't say, "Those are the kind of men who know how to love and cherish a woman. Those are the kind of men every woman should meet."

What if I were to ask a man caught in a homosexual lifestyle, "Tell me the first thing that comes to mind when I say evangelical Christian." While responses may vary, I'm pretty sure that he wouldn't say, "While they don't agree with my lifestyle, I've never felt such love and compassion."

We will never win our world for Jesus as long as this reality remains unchanged.

Most people are familiar with the *Mona Lisa*. But how many could describe its frame? The reason no one can remember the frame is that the job of a good frame is to complement its contents, not to draw attention to itself. In light of this illustration, what are people seeing when they look at you and me? Are they seeing Jesus, or are they seeing the frame of our humanness? I pray that they're seeing the One we've been called to exemplify: Jesus Christ.

Growing Up Ethnically Advantaged

I was born into a very large Italian family in Rhode Island, where the politically correct term for *Italian is ethnically advantaged.* To us, everyone else is ethnically challenged. Where I grew up, the rule was that everyone who was anyone had to be Italian, Catholic, and Democrat.

My family moved to Southern California when I was eight. My parents said we were going on a two-week vacation. Little did we know that we would never return to our home state. I found out later that my father had run into some financial trouble and was intent on making a new start.

At the age of thirteen, I acquired a part-time job at Standard Brands Paint Company sweeping floors and stocking shelves. Between work and family, I had some pretty awful role models. At work, I learned all the wrong ideals: how to stay out late, chase women, and drink to excess. At home, I learned a lot about life from Uncle Louie. I know it sounds like a cliché for a guy from a big Italian family to have an Uncle Louie, but I did.

The only thing that kept me from getting sucked into that lifestyle was falling in love. Cindy and I were high school sweethearts and married shortly after graduation. But in tying the knot so quickly, we had unknowingly set the stage for disaster.

Trouble on the Home Front

With the added financial responsibility of marriage, I began to work forty hours a week at the paint store and enrolled in college part-time. During this time, Cindy's younger brother excitedly shared the news that he had just accepted Jesus Christ at a Campus Crusade for Christ meeting. His conversion deeply affected Cindy. I didn't know it at the time, but she had been quietly seeking the Lord for several months. When she saw the joy on her brother's face (a fellow who had previously been growing marijuana in the family's birdbath), she knew the change was real. Shortly thereafter, Cindy made her own personal commitment to the Lord. All I asked was that she leave me out of it.

From that moment on, our lives headed in opposite directions at an accelerated pace. Friends counseled Cindy to abandon the marriage. One person asked her why she stayed with me, because it was obvious that I would never become a Christian. But as time went by, I began to notice some changes in Cindy's life. Out of sheer curiosity, I agreed to accompany her to a Wednesday night Bible study at an old fraternity house near the UCLA campus.

The frat house was packed with young people, and we struggled to find a place on the floor to sit. Energy and excitement filled the air. Before long, a rough-looking man wearing a black leather jacket opened the meeting with his testimony. He told of his connection to the Mafia and his years with the Hells Angels motorcycle gang. Then he told how accepting Christ had changed his life. He completely blew my stereotype of what a Christian was. Then a man named Hal Lindsey spoke. He made the Bible come alive. Seeds were sown, but I wasn't ready to let them take root.

Jesus as Savior but Not Lord

A few months later, on my commute home from work, I reflected on my life. I had just been promoted to store manager in Pasadena. My company stock was booming, and I was in line for another promotion. However, I had an overwhelming sense that if I didn't get serious about God right at that moment, I might never have a second chance. As I sat in bumper-to-bumper traffic that afternoon, I prayed my version of the sinner's prayer: *Lord, if you are real, I want the kind of relationship with you that these other people have.*

When I got home, I proudly told Cindy what I had done. She was thrilled. She remembered the wonderful effect that conversion had had on her brother's life and couldn't wait to see the evidence of change in mine. Sadly, Cindy's optimism was soon crushed. Although I professed to be a believer, my life didn't change. I didn't read the Bible, pray, or attend church. What I did was accept Jesus as my Savior but not as my Lord.

During the next eight years, I did more damage to the kingdom of God as a new believer than I'd done before I knew God. At work I was promoted to district manager. Along with the title came responsibility for more than a dozen stores and hundreds of employees. The position also required a lot of travel, and as is often the case, time spent apart from family made way for temptation. My new executive lifestyle included drinking and adultery. My employees knew that I was a Christian, yet they were also aware of my lifestyle. I could hear them in the back room saying, "What a hypocrite." Followers of Christ must realize that they're constantly being watched.

Eventually Cindy uncovered my secrets. It was the first predicament that I couldn't manipulate myself out of. I was dangerously close to losing the people I loved most: my wife and my children.

You Told Him, Didn't You?

Over the next week or so, Cindy and I didn't communicate much. She waited on the Lord and sensed God telling her, *Be still and quiet. I am wrestling with Vince's soul.* At the time, she and the kids were attending the Church on the Way in Van Nuys, California. One Sunday, in an effort to find marital and spiritual healing, I decided to join them. About halfway through Pastor Hayford's piercing sermon, I turned to Cindy and said, "You told him, didn't you?" It was as if every word he spoke were directed to me.

After the sermon, Pastor Hayford asked the congregation to form small prayer circles. When one of the guys in my group asked whether I had a request, I let it all out. I thought that they would all be flabbergasted. Instead, they listened quietly and then prayed over me. It was incredible. I didn't know anything about the ways of the Lord back then, but the Holy Spirit was doing unbelievable things.

Soon after, Cindy and I began attending counseling sessions with one of the associate pastors. In the first appointment, we poured out our hearts and then waited for the counselor's response. He turned to Cindy and asked, "What are you going to do?"

"I don't know," Cindy replied.

"What did Jesus do for you?" asked the pastor.

Cindy's response came immediately. "He went to the cross."

"Then what?"

Cindy paused, then answered, "He died."

The counselor's next words reverberate in my mind even today. He turned to me and said, "Vince, I want you to look into your wife's eyes." I did so for an uncomfortable amount of time. What he said to me next cut me to my core: "I don't see much life in there. Do you?"

In that moment, God gave me a panoramic view of the incredible amount of pain that I had heaped on this precious child of his. I can't remember a time when I ever felt so ashamed. I repented for my sins and was incredibly grateful when my wife agreed to stay and work things out. She told me later that God whispered to her in a clear but inaudible voice, *If you will forgive Vince, I promise you there will be a third-day resurrection.*

A New Man

I was baptized soon after this event, and Christ reached down and washed me clean. For the first time, I was able to let go of my past. I felt like a new man. With a newfound sense of conviction, I made a habit of studying the Bible and incorporating God's Word into my life. The Lord became my spiritual CEO.

Things at work took off as well. After thirteen years at the company, I was named corporate vice president. But before long, the company's business philosophies began to change. In an effort to avoid a hostile takeover, several of us met on the top floor of a Los Angeles skyscraper with scores of lawyers, bankers, accountants, and company executives to sign for a $200 million loan. The interest payments alone were staggering. At that moment, we made some serious mistakes as leaders.

In the midst of all this turmoil, I remember praying, *Lord, you must have something else for me.* After much time in prayer, God led me to a Christian man who happened to be looking for an executive vice president to help him merge with another ministry. I agreed.

As a businessman, I had been used to dealing with all nationalities, but every management tool I possessed was worthless when it came to trying to get two religious cultures to come together. It was ugly, and I learned how helpless I was. The only effective tool was prayer.

Consulting God's Word

In today's culture, we are mired in our superficial approach to Christianity. We will never discover God's vision or have the ability to live it out unless we are intimate with him. I used to convince myself that I had done my spiritual duty for God by going to church. Coming together with a community of believers is necessary for spiritual growth, but it should never take the place of our time alone with God.

What should we do during that time alone? One thing we need to do is read his Word. Joshua 1:8 says, "Keep this Book of the Law always on your lips; meditate on it day and night." Matthew 22:29 says, "Jesus replied, 'You are in error because you do not know the Scriptures or the power of God.'"

When they first came out, home computers arrived with a healthy-sized owner's manual. The original writer of the computer programs knew that we wouldn't be able to figure everything out, so it was written down for our use. But if you're anything like me, you don't need that silly manual—you can figure it out all by yourself.

In my house, the manual ended up on the top shelf, next to my Bible. And for a while everything worked just fine. That is, until I wanted to try something more difficult. Then I got the blue screen of death. Immediately I called for technical support. When I explained what I had done, the representative told me to follow the directions on page 94 and the problem would be fixed.

Can this illustration be applied to our lives? Just like that computer, we have been manufactured. Someone wrote our code and knows exactly how every part of our programming is supposed to function. Then he placed us on earth and provided us with a manual: the Bible. But often we treat it the same way I treated my computer manual—we don't refer to it until we're in trouble.

As Psalm 119:105 says, "Your word is a lamp to my feet and a light to my path" (ESV). If we choose to live in God's Word, it will illuminate our daily walk.

08

Bill McCartney

Dwight's Insight

In the summer of 1989, I asked Bill McCartney, then the head football coach at the University of Colorado Boulder, to speak at a Fellowship of Christian Athletes fundraising banquet in Southern California. The next morning, as I was taking him to the airport, he said he would really like me to pray for a special men's group that he and Dave Wardell were trying to get started. I asked him what they were going to call the group, and he said they didn't have a name yet.

As he was getting out of my car, I gave him a High Ground and Associates *newspaper to read on the plane. Two weeks later, Bill called to say that one of the articles in the paper had given him the name for their new men's group: Promise Keepers.*

—DLJ

Seeking God's Heart

The greatest longing of the human spirit is significance. We can spend our whole lives searching for that one thing that will make our lives worthwhile, yet if we don't find it, we feel lost, useless, meaningless. I have discovered where true significance lies. It's in seeking and finding the very heart of God.

Think about this: In nearly every area of life, someone has an advantage over you. Some people have greater intellect. Some people have greater economic resources. Some people are more physically imposing. Some people are more physically attractive. Some people have more experience they can draw on.

But in God's wisdom, there's one area where no one has an advantage—not even an inch—and it's the area that's the most important. God has said, "You will seek me and find me when you seek me with all your heart" (Jer. 29:13).

It doesn't matter what color, sex, or size you are or what your background is—it doesn't matter. Do you want God's heart? That's all that matters. And anyone who wants the heart of God can have it. When we have it, our lives take on full meaning and purpose.

What does a tree do? It gives oxygen, fruit, and shade. What does the sun do? It marks the seasons, separates day and night, and lights the earth. Just as all of God's creation has a special, significant purpose, so does every individual. When we enter into that pursuit of the heart of God, we're capable of living our highest purpose and finding true significance.

Why did Jesus pray for forty days and forty nights? He wanted God's heart. He was after the very heart of God. He was the Son of God, and he craved intimate fellowship with the Father. In his thirst for his Father's heart, Jesus set an example for us.

My Awakening to Racial Pain

Teddy Woods was not even fifty when he died suddenly of a heart attack. I didn't know him very well—just enough to say hello—but he had played football at my university before I was head coach. I knew who he was, and I knew this was a great loss, so I thought I would pay my respects as a head football coach and go to his funeral.

I'll never forget the day I walked into that church. The congregation was nearly 100 percent African American. The church was full, and the only seat I could find was way up in the front, in the very first pew. I was aware that a lot of the people there would know who I was, and I tried to be inconspicuous as I walked to the front.

The service didn't start right away—there was just some music playing. But as I listened to it, I began to choke up. I couldn't help myself—I got tears in my eyes. Then when the service started and people began to speak, I just lost it.

It was odd—people close to the family knew that I didn't know Teddy well—but here I was, carrying on. I was just sobbing and worrying that the family was thinking I was making a grandstand show of some kind. The entire service simply broke my heart.

I walked out of the church and knew that I needed to get in touch with that pain. I had been coaching African American kids for years and had been in their homes all across the country. I had been in ghettos. I had seen the circumstances these great young athletes came out of. But I never understood the pain they were in. So I started to read, and I started to ask African American guys I knew to explain things to me. It was very difficult for them. As I read and as some of them opened up to me, I began to come in contact with oppression—real racial oppression.

The Beginning of Promise Keepers

A colleague and I invited seventy other guys to fast and pray about this. Interestingly, we invited only white guys. That's who we knew. I don't think there was a single African American present that day when we gathered to see what God wanted to do in the hearts of men across this nation. That was the beginning of Promise Keepers.

The following year, more than four thousand men were in the basketball arena in Boulder, Colorado. I gave my testimony, and we had a long program. It was a supercharged event, beyond anything any of us had ever experienced. Then it was time for me to close out the event. All I was going to do was get up and say that if each guy would bring twelve others, we could fill the football stadium next year. I was going to say, "Your responsibility is to bring twelve guys. You've got twelve months." But just before I got up to the podium, I felt the Spirit of God say, *Wait a minute. Look at the panorama of people here. What do you see?*

"I see guys who love Jesus," I said.

What else do you see? the Spirit asked.

Finally I got it. "I see all white guys," I said.

The Lord said, *You can have fifty thousand here next year, but if you don't have a full representation, I'm not coming.*

So that's what I told the group. It didn't seem consistent with the Scripture verse that says, "Where two or three gather in my name, there am I" (Matt. 18:20), and people challenged my words, but I simply spoke what God had put in my heart.

The next year, I started going outside Colorado to talk to men about what God had put in my heart. But I'm not a preacher; I'm a reacher. I'm a guy who has a passion for the gospel of Jesus Christ, but I'm not given the kind of revelation that preachers have. The only way I can get up to speak is if I go into a prayer room and close the door and go after God's heart. As I would do that, I would write down what he gave me.

The message he gave me made me weep. My response was much more out of control than it had been at that funeral in Denver. I just wept over and over as I wrote the message about the damage of the oppression born out of our country's racial hatred.

Just Be Obedient

I went to five cities: Dallas, Indianapolis, Denver, Anaheim, and Portland. In Indianapolis, fifteen hundred men packed the church. When I walked in and sat down, a sixty-year-old guy stood up and yelled, "It's the greatest day of my life, Coach!" When they introduced me, there was so much excitement in the room that they gave me a five-minute standing ovation. It was unbelievable.

Then when I spoke the message that God had put in my heart, it was like a pin in the bubble. It burst everybody's excitement. When I was done, people just sat there, sober.

I got several letters saying, "What right do you have to come and talk to us about these things? You weren't advertised to come and say things like this. I traveled two hundred miles to hear what you had to say about Promise Keepers, and instead, you gave us *that*. What a disappointment."

I went back to my prayer room. *Lord, where did I miss it? But the answer I got was this: Just be obedient.*

So I continued to travel to other cities and share the message God had given me, and I received the same response.

Then I went to Portland. When I got into town, the guys who picked me up at the airport said that they had just had a Billy Graham crusade there, the greatest of all time, they said, and they wanted me to know that there was no problem in Portland with racial reconciliation—it had all been solved, they said. I took them at their word but still felt that God had given me a message to deliver to them.

Inside the church was the same feeling as had been in Indianapolis, an electric, supercharged atmosphere. And when I spoke, the same thing happened. They just sat there, looking at me, when I finished. I knew then that, regardless of what the guys had told me at the airport, Portland wasn't any different from anywhere else.

Then a guy walked up to the podium. It was unorchestrated, unannounced. He was a very distinguished-looking, older African American, a preacher. He was a guy whom everyone knew, and he had the respect of the people in the room.

For the longest time, he stood at the podium, tears coming down his cheeks. Finally he said, "I never thought in my lifetime that I would hear from a white man what this guy said." Then he said these four words that made my spirit resonate in a way that it hadn't for months: "Maybe there is hope."

When he said that, the Spirit of God said, *You are speaking exactly what*

I asked you to speak. You have heard from me. Ever since that moment, I have known a greater portion of what God is doing.

When John the Baptist heralded the first coming of Christ, he called men to repentance, and Scripture tells us that those who heard the message were convicted and were sorrowful for their sins and had a new determination to live holy lives. That response is similar to what occurred with Promise Keepers. Wherever we went, there was true sorrow for sin and a new hunger for holiness in the hearts of men. But remember what John the Baptist said to those guys: "Produce fruit in keeping with repentance."

"What should we do then?" they asked.

And John the Baptist told them what righteousness looks like: "Anyone who has two shirts should share with the one who has none, and anyone who has food should do the same" (Luke 3:8, 10-11).

Micah 6:8 says, "He has shown you, O mortal, what is good. And what does the Lord require of you? To act justly and to love mercy and to walk humbly with your God."

Three Questions

Doing justice means seeing the need in others and responding to it. So, in that context, for years I asked God three questions every day. These questions were foremost in my heart. They still are part of who I am. It didn't matter when I woke up—even if it was in the middle of the night. God's Spirit came to me with these three questions:

1. Lord, what is your strategy to end racism?
2. What is your direction for Promise Keepers?
3. Lord, if I get an opportunity to speak, what would you have me say?

I believe God gave me the answers to these questions. I also believe the answer is going to disappoint you. The answer is the most underestimated activity in the church. It's the most misunderstood, overlooked, and neglected area of the church.

Almighty God is going to respond through prayer.

God has a perfect, holy, righteous will, and his will is set, but there's a problem. He has given man a free will. Every person has a free will, and God will not force his will on man. So God is waiting for man to ask him to do what he already wants to do. I believe with all my heart that God has a backlog of things that he is waiting on, but they won't happen until we pray and ask him to do what he wants to do.

Jesus said, "Again, truly I tell you that if two of you on earth agree about anything they ask for, it will be done for them by my Father in heaven. For where two or three gather in my name, there am I with them" (Matt. 18:19–20).

The problem is that we have misunderstood this verse. It means that when two are gathered by the Lord in harmony, in the same spirit, stripped, barren, coming before him with no agenda, no suspicions, no judgment, no unforgiveness in their hearts, no condemnation, when we come before the Lord that way, that's when Jesus will come, because that's when he can have his way.

When we come before the Lord and pray, *Lord, all my hope is in you. My opinions don't count. You alone have the right to evaluate another man's life and behavior*, it's in that context that God will move. And God is waiting for the church to stand together and ask him to do what he already wants to do.

True prayer is when you pray God's will back to him. That's when you have a spirit of prayer on you. When that happens, the only thing that matters to you is this: *God, tell me your will, and I will repeat it back to you. That's my highest calling in life.*

Matthew 6:6 says, "When you pray, go into your room, close the door and pray to your Father, who is unseen. Then your Father, who sees what is done in secret, will reward you."

Have you ever thought about what that reward is? Do you know what God desires to give us? It's much better than answered prayer. God knows what we need before we ask for it. So, when we talk about answered prayer, the reward isn't simply the things we're asking for. It's so much bigger.

Every time we secretly go to God in prayer, when we shut everybody and everything else out, he gives us a greater portion of his heart. We actually inch closer to the very heart of God. We move into a relationship where nothing in our human experience is anything compared with this.

This is life's real quest. If we will go after him, he will give us everything that is in his heart. He will give us his wisdom, knowledge, understanding, and power. Those are the gifts. That's the reward.

What does this kind of prayer look like? It's strenuous. It's work. But James 5:16 says, "The prayer of a righteous person is powerful and effective." When you know God's will, you can be fervent. When you're praying back to him what you already know he wants to do, that's real warfare against the enemy. Prayer is red-hot. Prayer is full of fire. Prayer is from the heart. When it melts down from the head to the heart, that's what makes a prayer warrior.

We serve a great God. We can't dream up a prayer request that he can't meet. And today, in this time of great strife, God is after guys who want his heart. And we can all have his heart. It is right there for us. All we have to do is go after it.

09

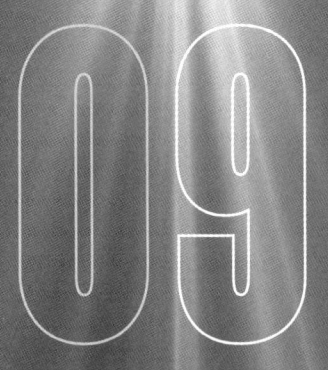

James H. Amos Jr.

Dwight's Insight

I met Jim Amos when a mutual friend suggested I welcome him to San Diego, where he had just assumed the presidency of Mail Boxes Etc. (MBE). During our visit, Jim told me about his experience with the US Marine Corps, specifically two duty assignments in Vietnam. He then went over to his bookshelf and pulled out a book titled The Memorial. He had written it to share the Vietnam experience as realistically as possible.

He was in the process of writing his second book, Focus or Failure: America at the Crossroads, when I met him. As he shared his concept with me, I started to understand his heart, which, for a macho, gung-ho marine, had great softness.

Jim remains committed to God, his family, and his community.

—DLJ

The Character of the Leader

Mountain climbers use pieces of equipment called pitons to help them scale peaks. Pitons are spikes fitted at one end with an eye for securing a rope. The spikes get driven into the granite or ice so that the climbers can put their weight on them and continue to ascend. Climbers trust these pitons with their lives.

In a world where we can't seem to count on much of anything, we need pitons we can hold on to. Life is a struggle, and we are all at times desperate for something that will hold us, something we can use to ascend to the next level. Sometimes we simply need pitons to keep us from falling. While there are many potential pitons to grasp, some are of more consequence than others. I can think of at least three.

The first piton is commitment. As part of the strategic planning process at Mail Boxes Etc. (MBE), our leadership council developed a statement of core values. One of the values we agreed on was commitment, and it subsequently went on the walls of offices and cubicles and hopefully into the hearts of those who served the MBE brand.

Yet if the value of something is determined by the way it's treated, then commitment isn't worth much today. It's cheap in marriage, cheap in business, cheap in politics, and cheap in athletics. We have lost our way and appear to have blurred the concept of commitment.

Some say that when conquerors entered a new territory, they sometimes burned the bridges they crossed, saying, "This is it—there is no turning back." That reflects a kind of commitment that we need to consider anew today.

Being faithful and committed isn't a function of personal convenience. I am well aware that I'm capable of lacking commitment when things get difficult. Yet I know that commitment isn't a function of self-indulgence, happiness, or economics. It's a function of doing the right thing, even if the cost is dear. As such, commitment doesn't appear to reflect the reality of our culture anymore.

Embracing a piton like commitment and applying it to our lives is a challenge that requires almost superhuman effort, especially when the popular approach to pain, frustration, and sacrifice is to simply walk away.

"God, Let Me Feel Pain"

I once read that people with leprosy can lose nerve endings and end up severely burning or cutting an arm, leg, or finger without knowing it. Consequently, the prayer of a leper is "God, let me feel pain." For them, pain is a gift from God. For me, it seems most of my life has been spent trying to avoid pain. But is it not in times of pain that we renounce selfishness, overcome the desire to avoid difficulty, and embrace humility? This is where things most despised by the world often become our greatest teachers. These painful situations are wake-up calls, teaching us to make the transition from follower to manager or leader. They are also where we learn what real strength is and the true definition of success.

If we want a picture of what true commitment looks like, we only need to look at Jesus Christ, who, as Philippians 2 tells us, followed his commitment to God all the way to the cross (v. 8). Is that not the ultimate example of bridge-burning commitment? Of course, he had opportunities to say, "This is too hard, too painful, too stressful," but he didn't.

I look at Christ's commitment, and then I look at my commitment to Christ, and I realize that I desire that kind of "don't look back" approach to faith. I want to keep looking forward, toward an eternal life in fellowship with God. Yet I also recognize how easy it is to fall away from this type of commitment when things get painful or stressful. I must look to the Lord as the example of bridge-burning commitment.

Today, instead of being encouraged to maintain our commitments to Christ or our spouses or our values, what we're taught is upside down and backward. When faced with a challenge, most people's dominant response is to cut and run. We're taught that the solution to pain, emptiness, or stress is found in a drug, an adult beverage, entertainment, or simply working harder. We don't want to be unduly stressed. We want to avoid pain.

Like the leper, we've lost our sense of feeling. Our nerve endings are gone, and we can no longer differentiate between joy and pain, wealth and poverty, good and bad, because we've missed the difference between truth and deceit. Christ took his commitment to the cross. We must do the same.

A Business's Highest Priority

In Greek there's a word that means "to sharpen, to engrave." That's where the word *character* comes from. Having character, the second piton, means being willing to take an unpopular position. As an example, I don't believe the number-one purpose of a business is to make a profit. Some people get very exercised about this. Imagine having a publicly owned company, sitting in a room full of investment bankers, and saying that profit isn't the company's top priority.

What I do believe is that the top purpose of a business is to build character in others, to raise people to a higher level of performance, morals, and overall excellence. Isn't that what Christ did with his disciples and with others he touched? Profits come and go, but character is eternal. Developing Christlikeness in one another is more important than making money. If we do this, it is my firm belief that profit will take care of itself, not just in the short term but in the long term as well.

Everyone has influence over other people every day. Changing lives and growing people should take precedence over making money. It's a cliché today to say that our biggest asset is people, but it's true. You've read the business reviews and the theoretical arguments about process and systems. The reality is that people run systems, not the other way around. We should be growing people, teaching character, values, and attitudes by what we say and do at home, at work, and everywhere else we go. Investing our lives in people brings the highest return.

The Importance of Words

Our words, the third piton, are the most powerful instruments and influences in the world. Words are seeds that are planted in the heart for good or evil. They are capable of echoing down through eternity. We have the opportunity to stand on the precipice of eternity and yell out, "I hate you; I hate you" or "I love you; I love you." Rest assured, what we yell out will return full force. Words presage deeds, and deeds reveal character.

As Lord Chesterfield said, "Words are the dress of thoughts."[1] They're containers filled with emotions and meaning. They're planted in hearts, where they take root and grow.

Words can convey affirmation and respect. Or words can ridicule and insult, belittle and dishonor. Words can tear apart relationships and, ultimately, the very fabric of tradition and history. Our character can be seen by our choice of words, which is evidence of the attitudes and motives of our hearts. We have power to speak life or to speak death. What words should we speak?

The gospel of John begins, "In the beginning was the Word, and the Word was with God, and the Word was God" (1:1). The Word that John described is Jesus Christ, and the word that we speak to one another can be the same. In the way that we talk to one another, we can be saying Jesus and reflecting him. How carefully do we choose our words? Do we speak Jesus, speak life, speak love to one another? I wonder what would happen if we realized that all our words are spoken coram Deo, "in the presence of God."

We don't need to use an abundance of words to speak life and love. For example, just six words can be powerful. How about "I admit I made a mistake"? Tough to admit but essential in relationships. "You did a good job" can be profound. As hard as we try to honor people and celebrate their success, it's clear that people can't get enough praise. The human spirit is desperate for affirmation.

"What is your opinion?" can make all the difference. You don't hear that asked very much today. What are perhaps the three most important words we can speak? "I love you." Our lives are defined by the people who choose to love us and by those who choose not to love us.

Two words of significance are "Forgive me." We can't pass through this life without needing a ton of forgiveness. Every enduring relationship requires it.

These three pitons—commitment, character, and words—are ways in which we reveal our trust in Christ to the world. They enable us to assist in transforming hearts one person at a time. They offer support for the journey—the climb toward eternal life in Jesus Christ.

10

Hank Brown

Dwight's Insight

Hank Brown is a man who has used all the talents that God has given him to weave a tapestry of success in his life. My relationship with Hank goes back to his mom and my mom being in each other's weddings.

In 1980, Hank won a seat in the House of Representatives and served five two-year terms. He was then a US senator for six years.

Hank had the opportunity to help develop a major role for the University of Denver in international trade, and then the University of Colorado asked him to step in as interim president, a job that became permanent in 2006 until Hank's retirement in 2007.

—DLJ

The Role of Challenges in Our Lives

*L*eadership is one of those words that everyone uses, but not everyone agrees on its definition. Some people believe leadership involves articulating a vision and then searching for a following. Christians believe leadership involves letting others see Christ at work through them.

Leadership involves listening to others. By *listening*, I mean actively seeking out what other people think about a subject, not just having the people closest to you tell you what they think you want to hear. Leadership begins with listening and thinking.

One of the misconceptions people have about leadership is that the leader has everything figured out and knows exactly where the organization is going. As a result, some have wrongly followed spiritual leaders who had simple answers to what it means to live in this world. For instance, some have taken the commandments that God gave Moses and the admonition that Christ gave us to love one another and have made them into a formula for gaining prosperity in this temporal world.

The thought is that if we abide by the Ten Commandments and if we do what Jesus told us to do, then God will reward us with earthly treasure and protect us from tragedy. But what is our Maker's purpose in guiding us? Is it to guide us toward prosperity in this world or the next?

The Tragedy at Columbine

The incomprehensible tragedy at Columbine High School in my home state is an example of a tragedy that has affected not only the families of the victims but all of us as well.

Next month it will be forty-six years since my brother died in a gun accident. He was only sixteen—the same age as several of the children who were murdered at Columbine. My mother told me that not a day went by that she didn't think of my brother and miss him. I suspect that the parents and other loved ones of the victims at Columbine do the same. The memory of those children will be with them every day for the rest of their lives. How do we explain it? How do you reconcile the tragedy in your own mind?

We believe our God is good; we believe our God is love; we believe our God is all-powerful and capable of controlling everything. How, then, could something this evil be allowed to happen? It's not a new question. It's been with mankind throughout history.

The Story of Job

A few thousand years ago, Job had the same question. He was devout, religious, and pious. He was committed to carrying on the work of the Lord, yet great tragedies were visited on him. He lost his fortune. He lost his health. He even lost his beloved children. But he didn't lose his faith. And throughout his suffering, he asked, "Why?"

Was he being tested? Was he being punished? His friends suggested that he was being punished, that he must have done something wrong. Yet Job was a righteous man. He hadn't been evil; he hadn't sinned. He'd kept the faith. His friends' attitude is perhaps parallel to the way many of us think. It's natural to think that if we're good, if we follow the rules, good things will happen to us. And yes, if we sin, we'll be punished. Yet Job hadn't sinned. I don't pretend to know the answer. But I want to suggest that part of the answer lies in God's purpose for our lives in this world.

What if this earthly existence is not intended to be a paradise? What if our Maker's real kingdom is not of this world? What if the purpose of our earthly existence is to train us, to prepare us—not for this world but for the next? What if the commandments of Moses and the admonition to love one another aren't a formula for prosperity in this world but are guidance for how to behave when we truly accept grace? Not a way to earn grace, but a prescription for how to live if we accept grace. What if those commandments are the best advice in history on how to live a joyous life and find happiness on earth?

If this is so, then our earthly existence may not be about earning our way to heaven or even enjoying a perfect life on earth. It may be about learning and preparing for the next life.

Preparing Our Children

Parents love their children more than life itself. But do we do their homework for them? If we don't help them with their homework, they may fail and may not have the chances we hope for them. But if we do their homework for them, what do they learn? How do they learn that they have to prepare in advance for the next challenge? How have we helped them learn a lesson for life?

Growing up, I couldn't understand my mother. How could she be so tough? She never once bought the stories I brought home about how everyone did it, how it must be okay because everyone else got by with it. In fact, she was never even tempted by them. I recall several times when she forced me to confess my sins—once to a store owner from whose store I'd taken some gum, once to my grandmother, and once at school. Those forced confessions resulted in unbelievable embarrassment. How could she do such a thing?

If I wanted something, her answer was "I'll help you find a job." I worked twenty to forty hours a week while I was in high school; in the summers I had one or two full-time jobs, depending on the summer. My parents were divorced. Mom worked full-time. She didn't have a lot of time to supervise me. But her strategy was to keep me busy, and she kept me so busy I mostly stayed out of trouble. As I look back, I wonder whether I have been near as good a parent as she was.

He Was the One Who Loved Me the Most

I will never forget the Clarence Thomas confirmation hearings—I was serving in the US Senate then. I recall a question posed by one of my colleagues—a person of great integrity—who had strong doubts about Clarence Thomas's judicial philosophy. When his turn came to ask questions, the senator said to Justice Thomas, "I see two Clarence Thomases, not just one. I see one that seems so kind, generous, thoughtful, and warm. And then I see one that is mean, cruel, and hard. Which one are you?"

Justice Thomas responded immediately. "There is only one Clarence Thomas, and I am he. I used to wonder how my uncle could pretend to care for me so much and be so hard on me. It wasn't until later in life that I learned that he was the one who loved me the most. He loved me enough to prepare me for the challenges ahead."

I wonder whether our Lord's purpose is to prepare us for the life to come.

My grandfather gave me a wonderful little book by Woodrow Wilson called *When a Man Comes to Himself.* It had as strong an influence on me as any book I've read. Wilson, as you may know, was an idealist. In the book, he talked about the true joys in life. He observed that the real pay one gets from a job isn't the paycheck at the end of the month, although that's important. The real joy comes from what you do. A bricklayer or carpenter can drive through town and see the homes he's built that provide shelter and warmth for families. Others can look at the work they've done and see how it affects the lives of the people they know. Wilson's thesis was that you are what you do with your life. He believed that "a man is the part he plays among his fellows."[1] If that's true, it's worthwhile for us to ask ourselves from time to time what our lives are amounting to.

Wilson's thought was that we are the sum of our relationships with others. Perhaps that's a good guide as we evaluate what we do in life. It's also a pretty good guide as we examine whether we've found real joy.

I don't know the answer to Job's question. As it does you, the currents of evil in the world trouble me. Like you, I suspect that our responsibility is to do what we can to prevent tragedy. I'm not sure there's a surefire formula for doing that, but I do believe that the freedom God gives us to live our lives and make our choices surely must be designed to prepare us for another world and help us understand that we have a role in making this world better.

11

Bill Armstrong

Dwight's Insight

Bill Armstrong was a gifted businessman who served in the US House of Representatives for six years, then in the US Senate for twelve years. It was while Bill was serving in the House that he became a Christian. In 1991, Bill returned to private life, where he immersed himself in a Colorado mortgage company.

I met Bill at a political outing. I believed then and I still believe we need more businesspeople in politics—people like Bill.

He passed away in 2016.

—DLJ

The Significance of Spiritual Leadership

I had the privilege of closely working with many talented, outstanding, dedicated, celebrated men and women in Congress, the cabinet, the White House, and the federal courts for nearly two decades. Interestingly, however, I don't know of one of them who would say that within their vocations they had discovered the answers to the deepest questions of life.

On the other hand, I know many—perhaps hundreds—of these celebrated men and women who would solemnly testify, as do I, that you can't discover what's really important in life through military strategy, economics, political science, or any theory. They would affirm with me that you can find the answers to life's deepest questions only in a relationship with Jesus Christ.

One of these noted men was Dr. Charles Malik, a Lebanese statesman, educator, and diplomat. Near the end of his long life, this great Christian man put into words what many people in public and private life have concluded: "The needs of the world are much deeper than political freedom and security, much deeper than social justice and economic development, much deeper than democracy and progress. The deeper needs of the world belong to the sphere of the mind, the heart, and the spirit—a sphere to be penetrated with the light and grace of Jesus Christ."[1]

How is this a leadership principle? It seems to me that one of the responsibilities of leaders is to show people where they can find the answers to their questions. In this case, it's showing them where to find the answers to the most important questions.

Elected to Congress

After spending a decade in the Colorado legislature, I decided it was time to withdraw from public life and go back into business full-time. But just as I was making this decision, the census came along and a new district was created in the US House of Representatives. I threw my hat in the ring, and the good people of the Fifth Congressional District elected me to go to Washington to represent them as a member of the House.

By then I had reached all my goals. I had set a target of how much money I wanted to make by the time I was thirty and had achieved that. I had a fine family, a nice house, and some businesses, and I had served on some boards. Now I had been elected to the US Congress, to go to Washington and whisper advice in the ear of the president of the United States. Can you imagine how it felt to have achieved this level of success?

Actually, even though I had achieved all the things I had dreamed of, the things I knew were important, I didn't feel successful. In fact, I felt terrible. Inside I was crumbling.

A Stranger's Question

That was my frame of mind when a man came to call on me. He wasn't a clergyman or a constituent—just a dentist from Alabama who came to my office in the Cannon House Office Building. He asked me a completely unexpected and somewhat-confrontational question: "Bill, where do you stand with Jesus Christ?"

In retrospect, it's interesting how this situation turned out, because his question was a little embarrassing—and congressmen know how to get themselves out of embarrassing situations. I had a perfect opportunity to terminate this conversation, because as we were talking, the bells rang and the lights on my wall lit up to signify that a vote was about to occur in the House of Representatives. All I had to do was say to this guy, "Look—I've got to vote. Thanks for dropping in."

But for reasons I didn't understand but that now are absolutely clear, I didn't say that. Instead, I said, "I've got to vote. Walk over with me, and then we'll go down to the coffee shop, drink a cup of coffee, and talk." So that's what we did. I voted, and then we went down into the Joseph Martin Dining Room, a little chamber under the House of Representatives.

This dear guy, who has become a wonderful friend, shared with me a little pamphlet called *The Four Spiritual Laws*. At the time, I didn't know that *The Four Spiritual Laws* distilled the essence of the New Testament's teaching about man's relationship to God. Nevertheless, this dentist began to tell me about it. As he read, he moved his finger under each word of this little pamphlet.

He said, "You don't become a Christian because you're an American or because you live in the suburbs or because you're a member of a church or because your family members are Christians. Becoming a Christian is a choice. Would you like to accept Jesus Christ as your Savior right now?"

I really didn't understand the importance of his question. But by the grace of God, I did know the right answer and said, "Yes."

He said, "Fine. Let's pray."

We bowed our heads and said a little prayer. As I did so, without fully understanding what was transpiring, I became a Christian in the biblical sense of the word—that is, a person in whom Christ lives. I didn't understand until much later some of the significant details.

Then I had to go home and tell Ellen about this. That was a little awkward. It's not easy to go home and say to your wife, "By the way, today I had a life-changing experience in a public dining room with a man I never met before."

But we got past that. As a matter of fact, around the same time, Ellen recommitted her life to Christ. And we began to try to live with each other as a Christian couple and raise our children as a Christian family—only we didn't know much about how to do that. Our kids were doing fine. They weren't dropping out of school or using illegal substances or getting in trouble. But we realized we weren't providing them with the kind of spiritual leadership the Bible says Christian parents are supposed to give.

Just Like the Waltons

The first thing that occurred to me was that if we were to be a Christian family, we ought to all gather around the breakfast table and have a little Bible study every day. Much to the amusement of my children, that's exactly what we began to do. We developed this format: We would meet at the same time in the morning, starting with a little prayer. Then we would read something from the Old Testament (frequently from Psalms) and then pray again. Next we would read something from the New Testament. Then I would go to work, and the kids would go off to school.

When we began this family morning devotional, it was kind of a strange sensation. Somewhere I had gotten the notion that if you were a Christian family and you were going to pray together, you all should hold hands. So I proposed this. My son, Wil, was in kindergarten at the time. As we gathered around the table—my daughter, Anne; Wil; Ellen; and me—bowing our heads and holding hands, Wil peeked up and said, "Gee, Dad, just like the Waltons." Except it was more like the blind leading the blind. The reality is, we didn't have a clue about what we were doing.

Here is an interesting thing we discovered: God evidently doesn't care about expertise. He didn't seem to mind that we didn't know the buzzwords, that we hardly knew one end of the Bible from the other. We just knew we were in the presence of the living God and we were going to pray together. Since then, we have done this thousands of times. A lot of days it wasn't that much fun. Sometimes there was resistance from the children. Sometimes our hearts were hard. A lot of times there was tension, and other times we were too busy. But we just did it anyway, day after day, year after year.

Our children are grown up and have families of their own, so when we gather to pray in the morning, it's just Ellen and me and the dog. But I'll tell you, we have discovered the veracity of that old saying: "The family that prays together stays together." It has bound us together in a way that cannot be described.

12

Bob Shank

Dwight's Insight

My relationship with Bob Shank goes back more than thirty years. I have never known a man who has more God-given talents and gifts than Bob and who is also a good friend and confidant in so many ways.

Bob is the husband of Cheri and the father of two girls, and he has been the president of the largest mechanical contractor company on the West Coast as well as the senior pastor of an eight-thousand-member church in one of the most affluent communities in the United States. Today Bob is the founder and CEO of the Master's Program, which is dedicated to reaching out to businessmen who want to make a difference in the kingdom of God.

—DLJ

From Friend to Mentor

In a perfect world, families would be fully functional, fathers would play the role of mentors, and children would emerge into their adult lives with everything they need to fulfill their divine calling.

I was not raised in that perfect world—my family was fully dysfunctional. My father was never mentored, nor did he know how to provide that boost to his progeny. When I left home at seventeen, I was capable of surviving, but I lacked the potential to thrive.

The church our family attended had led me to a personal faith in the Lord Jesus Christ, and through my high school years, Youth for Christ helped me live my faith among my peers. My eternity had been secured through my salvation, but my future was murky.

Out on my own, I went to work and started college. I asked Cheri to marry me, and then her dad invited me to leave college early to join him in his business. He had four daughters, no sons, and no succession plan. To enter a twenty-five-year-old company with two hundred employees—and the chance to have a leg up in my career pursuits—was an offer only a fool would decline, and I was no fool.

He became, for me, the first in a line of mentors—in effect, surrogate father figures who deposited into my life the things that I needed in order to find and fulfill the purposes God always had for me. These mentors are the giants on whose shoulders I stand today.

Jack Kinney

Legally he was my father-in-law, but relationally he was the first patriarchal figure who saw potential in me. Jack and I had a common Christian faith, but his was manifested in his ethical business practices, while mine was more outspoken. He taught me how faith could be demonstrated in daily decisions that put doctrine over dollars, while I was allowed to position his company—our company—as an overt outpost of our biblical beliefs.

Jack's mentoring was an apprenticeship in Christian entrepreneurship in an industry that was far from holy ground. I had the rare opportunity to earn my degree in business in the corner office instead of in a college classroom.

I'm sure that all my promotions were merit based and not unduly preferential, but I was given the chance to run and build the business. Jack gave me his blessing.

Lorin Griset

Lorin Griset was a World War II hero, the nephew of William Cameron Townsend (founder of Wycliffe Bible Translators), the mayor of our city, a deacon in our church, and a national leader in various ministries, including the Christian Businessmen's Committee (CBMC).

As a young business leader, I caught Lorin's attention, and he took me under his wing. Jack had showed me how to do business as a Christian; Lorin showed me how to do ministry as a Christian businessman. Lorin's arm around my shoulder—while frequently twisting my arm behind my back—moved me along in the national CBMC network. Through his promotion, I became the chairman of our local CBMC chapter, emceeing the weekly breakfasts and, most often, closing those gatherings with an appeal to accept Jesus as Savior.

Lorin treated me as a son; he invited me onto an elevated platform of leadership in the national Christian community. He gave me his blessing.

Chuck Swindoll

My career had afforded me success, but it lacked the satisfaction of significance. While building the family business to a place of national prominence, I hired and coached a great team of leaders to whom I delegated authority and gave the chance to prove their potential. As the company expanded—and my management team grew—my time became more available for outside ministry roles. Cheri and I looked to the horizon and wondered what we wanted to do with the rest of our lives. Was God stirring us to ask some uncomfortable and possibly disruptive questions about our future?

Chuck Swindoll was a well-known pastor in our community—and a nationally respected speaker and author—but he was not my pastor. We were both involved in ministry initiatives that took us outside the limits of our respective churches. He was a safe and respected person with whom I could be completely vulnerable and have an honest conversation about the rest of my life.

Our relationship went from respected friends to mentor/protégé as our interaction informed a massive transition—from for-profit business leadership to nonprofit ministry to business leaders—that would change the course of my future.

Chuck's personal transparency was an exemplary demonstration of mentoring that marked my life. He continued to be available in the days that followed, allowing the voice of God to speak through him at crucial moments. He gave me his blessing.

Howard Hendricks

Howard Hendricks was a longtime professor at Dallas Theological Seminary, instructor to hundreds of pastoral and ministry leaders, and mentor to scores of key difference makers. I met him in 1986 at a weeklong training conference for people who taught the Bible. The second day, Howie asked me to join him for breakfast, and that meal sparked a relationship that continued until his death in 2013.

He was a key voice in the life stories of some of America's most notable Christian leaders, but the energy he invested in our relationship was focused and generous. We lived time zones apart, but he was available whenever I needed objective wisdom regarding key directional decisions. Our relationship was reciprocal: he would call me for counsel when he was considering matters related to my experience and strengths. That was an awesome lesson in mentoring—the best mentors are still learning, even from those in whose lives they are primarily contributors.

With confidence that God had spoken to me through Howie, I said yes to an opportunity that forever changed the trajectory of my kingdom leadership. Howie gave me his blessing.

Bob Buford

I met Bob Buford two years after I stepped from my business-career past into my ministry-career future. He founded Leadership Network in 1984 to bring the model of peer-provided leadership development he had found in Young Presidents' Organization into the megachurch pastoral community. For over thirty years, Bob's creative initiatives in serving developing Christian leaders—from both marketplace and ministry contexts—earned credibility among the men and women who have shaped the faith community for a generation.

Bob's book *Halftime* disrupted Christian leaders in the marketplace with its subtitle challenge: changing your game plan from success to significance. In 1995, Bob asked me to create a ministry that would help leaders find and fulfill their kingdom calling. Together we provided the venture capital and sweat equity that launched the Master's Program, which has been my principal pursuit for over twenty years.

Over that period, Bob's role in my life shifted from friend to mentor. Bob gave me confidence about coming alongside leaders who were already best-in-class and helping them become even better. He gave me his blessing.

The Role of a Mentor

Mentors are not teachers, transferring reliable information from books to brains. Mentors are not short-term, goal-setting figures; rather, they see unrealized potential in their protégés. They don't come with the right answers; they come with the right questions, and they trust their understudies to discover the answers that align with the God-given uniqueness encoded into their spiritual DNA.

Mentors are, most often, filling in the gaps left by fathers who may have had good intentions but lacked the vision to bet on the not-yet-visible that is locked inside their next-generation apprentices. To put it in historic, biblical terms, mentors give their charges their blessing.

Because of the mentors in my life, I've found my kingdom calling: I mentor Christian leaders to help them explore, expose, and—ultimately—exploit their kingdom calling. I've created an organization that provides for them, through a systematic, holistic process, what God provided for me through a succession of mentors. Those mentors empowered me with the blessing that every leader needs in order to be fully maximized.

13

George W. Bush

Dwight's Insight

In the 1980s, I served as chairman of Colorado's National Business Consortium for Gifted and Talented Children. All state chairmen were flown to Washington, DC, to meet with Vice President George Bush and Barbara Bush, who sponsored a reception at their home. That is where I was introduced to George W. Bush.

The next time I met him was when he addressed a Cinco de Mayo celebration breakfast. As he greeted a number of us, I told him that my wife and I prayed for him every night. He took my hand, looked me right in the eye, and said, "Thank you—your prayers are greatly appreciated and desperately needed."

Thank you, George and Laura Bush, for your willingness to be transparent leaders. Those of us who appreciated having a strong man of God in the most important position of leadership in the world appreciate your commitment.

—DLJ

When God Changes a Heart

The question posed to me by the moderator of the presidential candidate debate in Iowa gave me the opportunity of a lifetime. He was asking all the candidates to name the philosopher whom they most admired.

"Governor Bush, your philosopher figure?" he asked.

"Christ, because he changed my life," I replied.

The question was simple and straightforward, and I didn't hesitate to answer. But my answer seemed to send a shock wave through the halls of government. It seemed that all of Washington, DC, was asking whether a candidate for president of the United States could fly in the face of political correctness and testify to his religious beliefs, which included firm faith in Jesus Christ.

Pundits were quick to point out that I had committed political suicide. "Is this candidate out of touch with the American mainstream, or is he just a politician cynically pandering to the voters of the religious Right?" The answer was neither—I was simply saying that my faith is a fundamental part of my being. You can't separate faith from who you are. I was simply willing to admit that I was guided by a moral purpose that came from my Christian faith.

It turned out that it wasn't political suicide.

Only eight months into my presidency, the ruthless attacks on our country turned us away from our concerns about the economy and education and care for our families and forced us to confront a more complex world in which America was no longer safe from attacks. It was a chance to show that my faith was not just lip service to the idea of God but was a source of confidence and hope.

The moderator said, "I think our viewers would like to know more about how he has changed your life."

I said, "If they don't know, it's going to be hard to explain. When you turn your heart and your life over to Christ, when you accept Christ as your Savior, it changes your heart and changes your life. And that's what happened to me."

Some people seemed confused—even angry—about my comments. My expression of reverence for and deference to God struck a nerve in some. One magazine wrote, "It's one thing for a nation to assert its raw dominance in the world; it's quite another to suggest . . . that his presidency may be a divine appointment for a time such as this."[1]

I think many Americans are reevaluating their spiritual lives. I also think that moral clarity, which comes from faith, is precisely what the public is looking for in a leader, regardless of what the pundits and other politicians say. It seems that mainstream America wants leadership with strong moral and ethical character.

Wanting Something Different

After the attacks of September 11, an undercurrent of fear and doubt could be felt in America from the humblest church pew to the highest level of government. It was a time when the nation needed strong moral leadership that they could trust. From the outside, we were under attack from radical Islamic fundamentalist groups. But we were also under attack from the inside. It was a struggle between those who regarded their Christian values as vital for our nation's survival and those who viewed those values as obstructions to progress. The future of our nation depends on the outcome of this struggle, I believe. And this country has faced this struggle before. Our history includes examples of great leaders who found strength in prayer when they faced critical choices.

George Washington, our leader in the revolution, our first president, and "the father of our country," is thought to have said, "It is impossible to rightly govern a nation without God and the Bible." I believe in the power of prayer. In addition to prayer for the direction of this country and our world, I believe in the power of prayer for our coworkers and their families. Several times I stopped what I was doing in the White House or on *Air*

Force One and prayed for a member of our staff who was going through a difficult time. That's what people of prayer do. People don't seem to mind it. They seem to appreciate it. I don't see that as imposing my beliefs on others. I see it as saying that I care for them and so does God.

As much of the world already knows, I have not always been a man of faith and prayer. I was just another hard-drinking young man caught up in the boom and bust of the oil business in Texas. I was my seventh-grade class president, got straight As, played baseball and football, and was known as a popular kid with a big mouth. I was arrogant, aggressive, and sarcastic—not necessarily presidential qualities. My world was a combination of Texas bravado and the Ivy League culture of my father.

But in that environment, people accepted you for your word, your integrity, and how capable you were in your job. Politics was something people talked about, but most of the men and women I knew were not interested in things outside of Texas.

There were some dark days when I was a boy, particularly when I lost my sister Robin to leukemia. It is one of the starkest memories of my childhood. But I also felt my parents' pain and would do whatever I could to try to bring joy to my mother's face. I wanted to change the mood in my home, lift the depression. Perhaps it gave me the courage to try to do the same for my country after September 11.

Still, it took me a long time to accept my church's faith as my own. I spent many years chasing "the good life" of smoking, drinking, cursing, and carousing. But I was also calling myself a Christian. As Jesus said, "If a house is divided against itself, that house cannot stand" (Mark 3:25). Despite what I had been saying, I was far from God.

During our family vacations in Kennebunkport, Maine, we routinely invited Billy Graham to join us. We would all sit in the living room and ask him questions about religion and faith. It was a type of informal Bible camp for us. I could see God through Billy Graham's loving manner, and I was moved by it. I wasn't moved as much by what he told us during those times as by his character.

One night, after a particularly moving discussion, he and I took a walk on the beach. He asked me directly, "Are you right with God?" I said, "No, but I want to be." My whole life, I had been influenced by Christianity, but when asked this question, I could not say yes. After this talk, I was drawn to be different in my spiritual life. I wanted something real, and that's when my life began to change.

Faith Is the Framework

The night of my fortieth birthday, I had too much to drink and woke up the next morning with a hangover. I went out that morning for my usual three-mile run and decided that I was never going to take another drink. I told this to Laura when I got back from the run. Lots of drinkers make promises like this and then go back to binge drinking relatively soon. But I had made up my mind.

My faith helped me have the strength to change and become much more disciplined about my life. It helped redirect my life so that, instead of living for myself, I began to live for others.

As president, I made sure I had time every day for prayer and Bible reading; a physical workout; and talking with my daughters, wife, and parents. I tried to show my respect for the Oval Office any way I could. It's a type of sacred place for me because I believed I had a sacred trust as the nation's leader. So I made sure to wear a suit when I went in there, even during the evening or weekends. I also tried to have staff members show respect for one another by being on time for meetings and getting their work done on time.

Some people said that my Christian commitment was a threat to our Constitution and culture, but a person's religion is more than a church, a synagogue, a temple, or a mosque. Faith is the framework for living. It gives us the spirit and heart that affect everything we do. It gives us hope each day. It gives us purpose to right wrongs, preserve our families, and teach our children values. Faith provides us with a conscience to keep us honest, even when nobody is looking. And faith can change lives. I know firsthand because faith changed mine.

I was not interested in using my position as president to convert people to Christianity. I just wanted people to be better off. I wanted to serve them. That is why promoted what I call faith-based initiatives. A lot of religious groups and organizations serve the poor in their communities. I wanted to help them because I think our faith calls us to serve others.

In Washington, it was not easy to do that. Interpretations of how to enforce the separation of church and state created a lot of opposition from people who feared that we were imposing religious beliefs on the public. When I pray for God's direction, I do not see handwriting on the wall or hear an audible voice from God. I do sense the prompting of God in my heart, and I try to be attentive to those promptings. I want God's wisdom, and I need people to pray for me. We all need insight and counsel from others.

The Only Way to Live

Three days before we went to war with Iraq, I met with a young man who had the deadly disease cystic fibrosis. Laura and I talked with him and his family, and he told me about his life. Sam had chosen to deal with the disease by drawing closer to God, and he wanted me to know that. I gave him a baseball with the presidential seal on it, but he gave me an even better gift. He gave me a Bible with my name engraved on the outside. Inside was a bookmark to remind me to rely on God. He told me, "The only way to live is to rely on God."

I was not afraid to make my Christianity part of my public life. Neither were many of our leaders before me. John Adams "considered[ed] a decent respect for Christianity among the best recommendations for the public service."[2] And John Quincy Adams said, "The highest, the transcendent glory of the American Revolution was this—it connected, in one indissoluble bond, the principles of civil government with the precepts of Christianity."[3]

God has been a participant in our nation's public life from the beginning. Abraham Lincoln reportedly said, "I have been driven many times upon my knees by the overwhelming conviction that I had nowhere else to go. My own wisdom and that of all about me seemed insufficient for that day."[4] Dwight Eisenhower said, "Without God, there could be no American form of Government, nor an American way of life. Recognition of the Supreme Being is the first—the most basic—expression of Americanism."[5]

My relationship with God, through Christ, has given me meaning and direction. My faith has made a big difference in my personal life and in my public life as well. All our presidents, in times of calamity, turned to God for guidance. All I wanted was the courage to do what is right. Ultimately, I answer to him.

14

Dave Hentschel

Dwight's Insight

Dave Hentschel and I met at a retreat. I grew to admire his sense of humor and ability to laugh at himself. He had a huge job as CEO of Occidental Oil and Gas, which is one of the largest oil producers in the United States.

I had the privilege of having dinner with Dave and his wife one evening, and it was very apparent why he had been so successful as a husband and the father of three boys. Dave's consistency in what he does and whom he does it with says much about his heart for God and his desire to be available for God to use him.

—DLJ

Letting God Lead

Like many people, I chose to keep the Christian side of my life sectioned off from everything else. God was clearly in my life but not in control of my life. I eventually became more open as a Christian, and certain events helped bring that about.

After being with the Cities Service Oil Company for fourteen years, I was being considered for a promotion to the main office in New York. I had gotten to the point where the things that go on in major corporations—the politics in particular—no longer appealed to me. As I thought about my prospects and the process I was going through, I asked the Lord to take over my business life.

I got the job and continued to be placed in positions with more responsibility. I had so many jobs within the company that I decided no one in the firm would be able to tell whether I was performing well in each position, because I was never there long enough to even understand it myself. I truly felt the hand of the Lord moving me through this process more rapidly than my own abilities would have allowed.

I was also aware that I had probably moved past the Peter Principle level of incompetence. But I discovered something in the process—if you get three or four levels above your level of incompetence, you become competent again, especially with the Lord on your side.

Walking the Talk

During that time, I was not very open about being a Christian. Like many people, I chose to keep the Christian side of my life relegated to Sundays and Easter, if I was in town. If I was, then I was asked to give my testimony in front of three services at church. My immediate response was to find an excuse to avoid it. This response caused me to think about my relationship with Christ and how talking about it publicly might affect the way I conducted my life.

It became clear that what I said I believed, I had to live to the best of my ability. Nothing shows up faster and more harmfully than a Christian who really doesn't walk the talk.

My life had become very hectic because of pressures created by corporate raiders attacking the oil industry. Boone Pickens and a Canadian company bought large blocks of the shares of Cities Service in order to cause our company to be sold. Similar pressure was being put on another company, Conoco, so we entered into discussions about merging with them. But while the chairmen of the two companies were drafting an announcement about our merger, a hostile offer to purchase Conoco came out in the news media, and that ended our discussions. But because our merger discussions had been made public, it was clear that our company was now in play. After that, the only question was, Who was going to buy us?

Twice we were able to sniff out deals where Pickens tried to buy us, and both times we were able to take measures to cause those deals to fall apart. One of those steps was to tender for the control of Mesa Petroleum, the company Pickens ran. It was one of those crazy things you do in a tight situation—you tender an offer to a company you have no interest in and don't want at all, but it appears to be the only way to save your own company. Shortly after our move on Mesa, Gulf Oil tendered for Cities Service, but that fell through, putting us in a very bad place. By then, most of our stock was in the hands of arbitrageurs hoping to make large profits when the Gulf deal was completed. But when it fell through, the stock price dropped dramatically, causing the arbitrageurs to lose big money.

The next three weeks were crazy. The management of Cities Service had to tell the employees how everything was going to work out for the best, when in reality we had no clue how it was going to happen. That's when we were purchased by Occidental Petroleum, a company half our size, run by their chairman, Dr. Armand Hammer.

The first task I was given was to sell the refining and marketing divisions of Cities Service. I was running those businesses. But Occidental had no interest in those assets, so we sold them for more than $1 billion. Throughout that process, I considered what I wanted to do after the Occidental takeover. I was the third man in line, and it appeared that only one would be staying.

No one was more surprised than me when I was offered the job of chairman of Cities Service, which was to become the domestic arm of Occidental. As I thought about it later, it was just another time when God put me where I was supposed to be. The maturing process was continuing. A few years later, I was named CEO of Occidental Oil and Gas Corporation, the worldwide oil and gas operation.

The Influence of a Close Friend

During this maturing process, the Lord began to surround me with Christian friends. This may come as a surprise, but people at higher levels of corporations—especially if they have been at those corporations for some time—don't have many friends. The process of being CEO doesn't lend itself to being close to people inside or outside the company. If I define a close friend as someone you can talk to about anything and not be fearful that your confidences would be breached, then my list would have been two, in addition to my wife.

But that began to change, with amazing outcomes. While I was running the domestic company, Dr. Hammer asked whether he could send his grandson, Michael, to work in the company for about six months so he could learn something about the oil business. Michael had an MBA from Columbia and spent most of his life having a good time. He was still pursuing that interest when he came to Tulsa. After five months, Dr. Hammer asked whether I had ever heard of a person named Doug Mobley. I hadn't. Finding out who he was led me to a friendship that I will always treasure.

He read me a letter from Michael, in which Michael explained he had met a girl named Dru Mobley and had fallen in love for the first time. Dr. Hammer stated that Michael wanted to bring the girl to Dr. Hammer's house in Los Angeles for him to meet her, because he was very serious. Dr. Hammer wanted me to gather information on her father, Doug.

What I found out was that Doug was the most undisputed witness for Jesus Christ that I've ever known. His presence in the Hammer family would change some of them in dramatic ways. Michael and Dru got married but only after Michael had given his life to the Lord. You don't marry Doug Mobley's daughter without being committed to Jesus.

Dr. Hammer's brother Victor ran portions of the Hammer business. Although he was born Jewish, Victor claimed no religion, but he understood there was something different about Michael and Dru. After Victor became ill and stayed in the hospital for a long time, he moved to a Los Angeles hotel to recuperate. Doug Mobley was also in that hotel for a visit, and he felt a prompting from God to go visit Victor. During their conversation, he led Victor to Christ.

Victor went to the airport the next day and flew to Florida for some more rest, but he fell into a coma and died two days later.

This experience gave Doug a bridge to Armand Hammer, and Doug led Dr. Hammer into a relationship with Christ not long afterward. About a year later, when Dr. Hammer was dying, our prayer group prayed specifically for him. One of the guys in the group said, "Lord, please reveal yourself to Dr. Hammer this evening as he struggles between life and death." He died that evening. At his funeral a few days later, his doctor told us that she had put a picture of Jesus on his nightstand. He had been in and out of a coma, but that night, he leaned up toward the picture, pointed at it, and smiled—then he died. This occurred at the precise time we had been praying for him in Tulsa.

Six people spoke at Dr. Hammer's funeral: an attorney friend, a rabbi, a member of the Occidental board, a Catholic bishop, the mayor of Los Angeles, and Doug Mobley.

God Is Sovereign

Doug was instrumental in bringing me into fellowship with five or six other people who love the Lord, and my life would not be the same without them. We all had business problems, and we needed consultation, comfort, support, and, most important, the prayers of one another. Every time something came up, we could see the value of intercessory prayer and the interrelationships of men of like faith.

It was the support of friends like this that carried me through another harrowing experience. I needed to have some insurance forms signed by a local doctor, but because I had the good fortune of not being sick in Tulsa for fourteen years, I didn't have a local doctor. I took my annual physicals in Dallas. But these forms needed a local doctor's signature, so I called a doctor friend and asked for the favor. He said he'd do it only if he gave me a physical.

"I just had a physical in Dallas and will send you a copy," I said. No dice. So I went in to satisfy the requirement. That visit acquainted me with a test I had no previous knowledge about—a PSA test, which checks for the presence of prostate cancer.

My results were mildly elevated, so I was sent to a urologist for more testing. Five biopsies were benign, but the doctor wanted to follow them up with more tests. I found out later that he knew cancer was there—he just hadn't been able to find it. Three subsequent tests came out malignant.

I asked the Lord to lead me to the person who should do the surgery. I wanted it to be his person, not mine. I visited four surgeons—one at Mayo Clinic, two in Tulsa, and one at Johns Hopkins. When the doctor at Mayo walked into the room, even though I had heard of him only a couple of weeks before, I had the answer to my question. For the first time in my life, I stood in a room with a man wearing the exact same tie as me. And I had bought mine just two days before in Amsterdam. Coincidence? Not at all. Assurance? Definitely.

I relied on what had gotten me to that point: my relationship with Jesus Christ and my like-minded friends. I knew I was covered in prayer, and it gave me the assurance that, regardless of the outcome, God is sovereign. There is much I don't understand in the world, but I do know that for sure.

Making a Difference

I retired from Occidental after thirty-seven years, and I can honestly say I became busier than when I was working. I got involved in programs trying to eliminate sexual abuse of children, physical abuse of women, substance abuse, and domestic violence. What disturbs me about this is that, in Tulsa, there are churches on almost every block for twenty miles in any direction. They are good churches. They are great churches. But for some strange reason, the churches don't seem to have an impact.

These churches need unity of purpose if we are going to see some of these problems solved.

My life is very different now than it was when I was in the oil business. But this is where the Lord wants me. He wants to be in control of my life, not just in my life. That's what I want too.

15

Jerry White

Dwight's Insight

Jerry White was introduced to me at a gathering of Christian businessmen and their wives. I can honestly say that I don't think I have ever known a man who is more accomplished in his personal, business, military, and ministry life than Jerry.

Having been international president of the Navigators from 1986 to 2005, he continues to serve as the international president emeritus and chairman emeritus of the board and in that capacity has traveled around the world, encouraging people. One of the things I have noticed about Jerry is that he never complains. He loves and enjoys his family, and when he talks about how he and his wife, Mary, lost one of their children, he is so reverent and not resentful but is willing to share both the agony of the loss and the encouragement they received in order to go forward.

—DLJ

The Unexpected Journey

As a young air force lieutenant and mission controller, I heard countdowns dozens of times as I worked in central control of Cape Canaveral and the Air Force Missile and Test Center in Florida. This little kid from a small Iowa farm town and a divorced family sat in the middle of the burgeoning United States space and missile efforts, never having dreamed about more than finishing college and working at Boeing Aircraft Company.

"The mind of a person plans his way, but the LORD directs his steps" (Prov. 16:9 NASB) sums up the story of my life. Almost nothing of what I planned ever came to pass. In miraculous ways, God intervened and redirected my life—making it better but not always easier.

Humble Beginnings

I grew up in a rural Norwegian farming town in Iowa. Mother was seventeen years old and had dropped out of high school to raise me. Her marriage to my father didn't last long. In my first year he divorced her, leaving her in that small town with all the attending gossip that must have ensued. My young life was upended when my mother remarried and we moved to Spokane, Washington. My stepfather was a wonderful, gentle man. But he suddenly had a self-willed eight-year-old son.

Then God intervened. I got into a Sunday school class in a postwar housing-project community center led by a businessman, Bob Shepler. It was in that Sunday school class that I first clearly heard the gospel. Another layman, Walt Nelson, was helping Bob. On returning from a lake outing, Walt asked whether any of us wanted to pray to receive Christ as Savior. I did and knew that it was a clear commitment. That decision, followed by a further lordship decision in high school, set a new direction for my life. Bob stayed in my life for his entire life, demonstrating how an ordinary businessman can have an impact on another life.

I went to the University of Washington to pursue a degree in electrical engineering. At UW, I was introduced to the Navigators and to discipleship. In the middle of my sophomore year, I met Mary Ann Knutson, my future wife. We were married just before my senior year. I graduated with a BS in electrical engineering and a commission through the Air Force ROTC as a second lieutenant.

One day after graduation, we headed to San Antonio for air force pilot training. Life was really coming together. Assignments for pilot training in Texas, Georgia, then back in Texas brought us to another turning point. Near the end of my training, I failed a formation jet check ride. Never having failed a check ride before, I just assumed I would get another one three days later and all would be well. I didn't know the air force was cutting back on pilot numbers.

My orders came in for my next assignment at Patrick Air Force Base. I didn't even know where it was or what they did there. We packed up and drove to Florida. I then discovered that this was where the new American space program was based. The personnel officer told me I would be assigned to range scheduling. This sounded boring, and I told him so. With a bit of a smile, he said, "Lieutenant, just go check it out, and if you don't like it, we will find something else."

In retrospect, I was arrogant. It turned out to be the best assignment I could have wished for. As one of about five mission controllers, I learned about every type of missile being launched in this heyday of the early space program. It was 1960. Soon President Kennedy would announce that we would put a man on the moon in this decade.

Overextended

I worked long days and sometimes through the night, since launches and tests went on twenty-four hours a day. I met the first seven astronauts. I have a copy of a briefing agenda signed by Alan Shepard and John Glenn. This was heady stuff. I was reveling in it but neglecting my family. We had one son, Stephen. Mary took a job working for Pan American Airways, which ran the Atlantic Missile Range. I was working night and day, playing sports, teaching in the base chapel, and more.

One day I came home and Mary just blew up. "Marriage is not supposed to be like this." I was shaking but had no clue what she was talking about. We had had no marriage counseling, so we just bumbled along. I did my thing; she did hers—taking care of our child and working. Sadly, I hardly lifted a finger to help. I wasn't being a good husband or father. But her outburst got my attention.

Then I became ill, probably from stress and overwork. In the midst of all this, Billy Graham came to Patrick AFB for a one-night crusade. I was part of the follow-up committee. But it was another intense activity in an already-busy life.

At another point, Cleo Buxton, executive director of the Officers' Christian Fellowship, was in our home. He observed my schedule and challenged me: "Jerry, do you think you are trying to prove yourself for washing out of pilot training?" This was the first time anyone had confronted me on a personal, spiritual basis. I am not sure what my response was, but it was likely a denial. Even after all these years, I am not sure about the answer to his question. I was working hard. I was overextended. I did want to succeed. But that shot across my bow got my attention and caused me to examine my motives.

A Word from God

During this time, I did have a heart for God. I was studying Scripture, leading a Bible study, and sharing my faith. But I was frantically trying to prove myself and be successful. Our plan was to leave the air force and return to Seattle.

I haven't had many times in my life when I really felt I had a word from God. But one Saturday, I was out on my front lawn, talking to my neighbor. I asked him what his next assignment would be. He said that he wanted to go teach at the United States Air Force Academy. I asked how to do that. He said you needed a master's degree, good grades, and a special selection. God began speaking to me with a simple message: *Stay in the air force, get a master's degree, go teach at the Air Force Academy in order to reach out to students, and get more spiritual training from the Navigators.*

I immediately took the Graduate Record Exam and applied to the air force to be sent to graduate school. I received the discouraging reply that although I was qualified, they weren't sending lieutenants to grad school, at least not me. Mary and I prayed and decided to wait another year.

Starting Over

When my application was finally approved, we prepared to move to Dayton, Ohio, for graduate school, so we sent our goods ahead and traveled to Ohio with our two babies. We were sad to leave that exciting place but also relieved that we could start over in our marriage, family, and frantic life.

When we located an apartment, we called to collect our household goods. We found that everything we owned had been in a warehouse fire. Absolutely nothing was left. All we had was what we had packed in our small car, and that was not much. Suddenly we had to trust God's sovereignty in removing our material possessions, knowing that he wasn't trying to hurt us. We were shocked but knew that this was a new lesson for us, helping us loosen our grip on things.

I wasn't at all confident that I could meet the academic standards of a very demanding master's degree in astronautics. I worked incredibly hard, with Mary again carrying so much of the family load. But I decided to do all my studying at home, leaving the door open so the children could come in at any time. We were a growing family and were so very young. We remained in contact with the Navigators, though the nearest staff was sixty miles away.

After a year of graduate work, I had done very well, so I applied to the Air Force Academy. When I went for the interview, as I sat outside the door of the astronautics department, the executive officer came out of his office and introduced himself. "Oh, White? We have already hired you."

Open Doors

We moved to Colorado Springs and the US Air Force Academy in August 1964. I was now eager to embark on a new phase in my career as faculty and to see how God was going to lead. I had to wait only twelve hours.

We moved into temporary lodging at the academy on a Friday evening.

In the morning, I met with another faculty member who knew of the Navigators and with veteran Nav staff member Warren Myers. Warren had met with a couple of cadets, praying for the academy. The other officer had volunteered to help the chaplains work with cadets. They said they didn't need any help. But while we were meeting, the phone rang and it was one of the chaplains. He said they had too many cadets volunteering to work in the base Sunday school for kids, so they needed to offer them something else. He asked whether I would be willing to teach a Bible class for cadets. Would I? Of course.

The next morning, I met with five hundred cadets in the beautiful cadet chapel. I proposed a Bible class. Only a dozen or so came, but that was the beginning of a class that lasted about twenty years. Soon we had over eighty men attending. Our home on base overflowed with cadets on the weekends. At one point, Billy Graham came to Denver for a crusade, and the academy sent busloads of cadets. The TV cameras showed a sea of blue uniforms, and many responded to the gospel.

Unexpected Direction

Life was going very well. We loved the cadets, a somewhat slower pace of life, and getting help in our lives from the Navigators, which was headquartered in Colorado Springs. That tranquility was disturbed one day when my department head called me into his office. "We would like you to go get a PhD," he said. Right away, thinking of teaching and our ministry to cadets, I told him that I wasn't interested.

As I was driving home, the Lord spoke to me. *You didn't even pray about it.* The truth was, I didn't want to do it. I was afraid that I wasn't smart enough to do a PhD. And the air force would give me just two years to do it.

Mary and I prayed that evening. I was convicted that this could be God speaking. The next morning, I told my department head that I was willing to consider it. They gave me freedom to choose any university in the country. Again we prayed for the place of God's choosing. I prayed specifically that I would be able to do it in two years. Ultimately, we were led to Purdue University. I went there with fear and trembling, claiming Daniel 1:17 and 1:20, and got my doctorate.

Success and Suffering

Lorne Sanny interrupted my plans with an invitation to become executive director and COO of the Navigators. We again prayed and accepted this direction from the Lord. Then in 1986, to my astonishment, Lorne decided to step down, and I was selected to become the next international president. At the same time, the air force asked me to take on new responsibility as a general. I turned down the offer from the Navigators, thinking I had enough on my plate. I was especially concerned for our international staff, many of whom were in countries where the military was feared. After more prayer and consideration, I did accept the position and was also promoted to brigadier general.

Then all hell broke loose. On April 27, 1990, Mary and I were speaking at a conference in Ohio. Early in the morning, the phone rang. It was my executive assistant, Marjie Barnes. She hesitatingly said that the police had asked for our son's dental records. Steve had been shot late the previous evening. Our world was shattered. Our family picture was in the newspapers. Our daughters were frightened.

As devastating as Steve's murder was, we saw God work deeply in our lives as we had to trust his sovereignty and love for us. We had been part of a life group with three other couples for ten years at that time. They dropped everything and rushed to come to us. They literally took over our lives and helped us navigate those difficult days of police, publicity, and the memorial service. Our staff around the world and in our headquarters in Colorado Springs surrounded us with love and care. To our international staff, I went from being president and a general to being a hurting human being who desperately needed help, fellowship, care, and healing.

Looking Forward

In each of my subsequent military assignments, I have been able to share my faith. When I was promoted to major general, it was a surprise to me. Why would this little kid from the farm country of Iowa have this privilege? It all began when Walt Nelson and Bob Shepler led me to receive the salvation that Jesus offered. Life was never the same afterward. Since then, many of my family have come to faith in Christ.

As I led the Navigators for more than eighteen years, God blessed the ministry, expanding it into more than one hundred countries. Since I stepped down from that responsibility, God has continued to open doors in the air force and in a broader ministry of speaking and writing. I deserve none of this. It is all by the sovereign grace of God.

Today we are blessed with what really counts—three beautiful, committed daughters and their husbands and our grandchildren. Who could ask for more?

16

Tom Landry

Dwight's Insight

Forty years ago at the Fellowship of Christian Athletes summer conference, Tom Landry and his wife, Alicia, sat at our dinner table. Six years later, Tom was chairman of the FCA board and I was a board member. We became close friends.

It was Tom who first encouraged me to write a book about the importance of being transparent, and he promised to write a foreword for it. However, he became ill with cancer and died before we were able to get the book published.

Instead of using his foreword, I wanted to make his story its own chapter. The portions of this chapter on leadership and character are the strongest words that I have ever heard on the subjects. Tom truly was a transparent leader.

—DLJ

Faith That Overcomes Doubt

I played on some great teams in New York and loved living there. We had great success and won the world championship. I had achieved everything football could offer me. But I had emptiness and restlessness inside. Eventually my wife and I moved back to Dallas. Since I hadn't found fulfillment in climbing the ladder of success as an athlete, I figured I would find it in business. I told all of this to a friend who was a Christian, and he immediately knew what was wrong. He knew I was a churchgoer and not a Christian. My family had gone to church when I was growing up. I didn't have much choice since my dad was the Sunday school superintendent.

My friend, Frank Phillips, invited me to a men's prayer breakfast at a local hotel. He said it would be a few guys eating breakfast and studying the Bible together. I wasn't at all interested. But I couldn't think of a gracious way to decline his invitation, so I went. When I got there, I saw about forty businessmen gathered at tables for that week's study on Jesus's Sermon on the Mount.

I had never studied the Bible. I had hardly even read it. I found it confusing and irrelevant. But that morning, we read those chapters, and the men began discussing the meaning of Jesus's words. In the middle of my struggle to find direction and security in my life, the Bible was talking about those very issues. I was so surprised and intrigued that I went back to that Bible study the next week and the next and the next. I wanted to understand what else the Bible had to say. Using the same sort of scientific, analytical approach that enabled me to break down and understand an opponent's offense, I read and studied and discovered the basic message of the Christian gospel.

I realized that even though I had attended church all my life, I had never understood Christianity. I had been a spectator when God wanted me to be a participant. I had always been a good person, but here was the Bible saying I was as much a sinner as anyone in the world. All my life I had made my football career the number-one priority and let it dictate the direction of my life. But the Bible was saying I needed to make God and his will first and follow his direction for my life.

I had to decide whether I believed what the Bible said. All my other questions hung on that one. The more I read, the more it made sense, and the more I wanted to believe. Yet the analytical part of my nature kept asking questions and having doubts.

I can't point to a specific moment when I had a born-again experience. It took place over a period of months. But I finally reached a point where faith outweighed the doubts, and I was willing to commit my entire life to God. The decision didn't make an immediate visible difference in my life or transform me on the spot into a better person. But what my new Christian experience did was place football behind the priorities of my faith and my family, and it gave me a sense of confidence and peace about the future, whatever it would be.

I was in my thirties when I accepted Christ. And when God became first, my family took on a completely different dimension than it ever had before. As I began to understand what the Bible taught about loving God and my family, it helped me put football and winning and losing into perspective. It didn't make me want to win any less, but I realized that whatever I did or didn't accomplish as coach of the Cowboys wasn't the most important thing in my life. That helped take some of the pressure off.

Faith and Work

After I made my commitment to God, I looked for ways to incorporate my faith into my daily work and life. Soon after taking over as head coach of the Cowboys, I appointed Christian players to lead voluntary chapel programs and to invite guest speakers for a short morning service before our Sunday games. I also encouraged the beginning of a weekly couples' Bible study for players as a means of building spiritual and family values. While some of my assistant coaches and their wives joined the players at these Bible studies, I didn't attend them for the same reason I didn't lead or speak at the team chapel services: I wanted to be careful not to abuse my authority as head coach to push my own beliefs down the throats of my players.

At the same time, I never tried to hide what I believed. I regularly shared appropriate Bible verses in talks during team meetings. And every year at training camp, when I met with incoming rookies for the first time, I would share the story of my own spiritual pilgrimage, including what I'd learned about priorities.

I found that the only way to make my family the priority I wanted it to be was to give it priority in my regular routine. I was able to watch my son play football and my daughters do cheerleading. My wife, Alicia, and I went out as a couple one night every week. I tried to eat breakfast with my children every day before they left for school. And no matter what was going on at the office, no matter how much preparation remained to be done before Sunday, I always went home for dinner with my family. A lot of nights after dinner, I disappeared into the den to watch more game film, but whenever one of my daughters knocked on the door and asked, "Are you busy, Daddy?" I'd turn off the projector and say, "I'm never too busy for you, sweetheart."

I wasn't a perfect father or husband. But I was a much better person to live with than I would have been if God hadn't shown me the need to reorder my priorities. Fortunately, God was as patient with me as my wife and kids were when I would succumb to a serious case of tunnel vision and temporarily lose sight of everything but football.

Another important aspect of my spiritual life was my involvement with the Fellowship of Christian Athletes, which presents the message of Christ and challenges athletes to put those life-changing values into practice in their own lives. My being a professional football coach gave me a platform to speak to thousands of young athletes about their physical and spiritual needs.

During my early Cowboys days, my exposure to the great people working in Christian organizations like FCA and the Billy Graham Evangelistic Association provided me with an invaluable spiritual boost. The more-experienced Christians I met there inspired and challenged me to become more consistent in applying Jesus's teachings to my life. It was through the influence of these people that I became convinced of the importance of establishing the habit of setting aside a daily time for Bible reading and prayer.

A New Chapter

When I was fired from the Cowboys in 1989, since the new owner had his own coach in mind, I thought about the low points I had experienced as a player and a coach. This was the biggest. Worse than any playoff loss marking the sudden end of a season. After this, there were no more seasons.

I couldn't think only about the past. I immediately had to face an as-yet-unimaginable future. For that, I knew I would need and could ask for God's guidance and help—as I'd learned to do so many times before. I could never have imagined that the weeks and months to come would hold the most satisfying, most rewarding, and most incredible days of my life.

The restlessness I had at the beginning of my career was long gone. Saint Augustine prayed, "Our heart is restless until it rests in you."[1] Perhaps the highest praise I have heard was from a player who said, "I'd rather see a sermon than hear one any day. I'd rather someone walk with me than merely show the way. That was Coach Landry's method. He lived his Christianity."

A Commitment to Excellence

Coaching and leadership have the same basic rule in common: get people to do what they don't want to do in order to achieve what they want to achieve. The challenge of any great leader is to get the absolute best out of people.

If I had to pick my greatest strength as a professional football coach, I'd say it was innovation. But it started with preparation and knowledge. As a leader, you have to understand the present system, situation, or problem you're faced with before you can react effectively. If you're not one step ahead of the crowd, you'll soon be a step behind everyone else.

Every organization and every leader must have a clear philosophy or a statement of what you believe. It can provide a powerful sense of unity for everyone in the organization. And it is the leader's responsibility to make sure everyone buys into that philosophy. Out of that philosophy must come shared goals. I don't believe you can effectively manage people without helping them understand where they fit into the goals of the organization.

Leaders face adversity. It is so much a part of leadership that your reaction to adversity will determine your success or failure as a leader. It is partly a matter of attitude. Difficulties are challenges to overcome rather than problems to worry about. Leaders can't afford to look back and get too upset about past mistakes. They have to focus on what they will do differently next time. Leaders always have others watching to see how they react when things go bad.

The way leaders stay in control of themselves is by having confidence in their basic philosophy. Leaders have to be able to think clearly under pressure, which means they depend even more on their preparation. Leaders will be criticized for making both the right decisions and the wrong ones. They must be willing to listen to criticism and make changes. Or not. The trick is in deciding which to do when. Perhaps the most important step in dealing with criticism is realizing it's part of the job.

Character Matters

I've seen the difference character makes. Give me the choice between an outstanding athlete with poor character and a lesser athlete of good character, and I'll choose the latter every time. The athlete with good character will perform to his fullest potential and be successful, while the athlete with poor character will usually fail to play up to his potential and often won't even achieve average performance.

In my opinion, character is the most important determinant of a person's success and ability to handle adversity. Most of a person's character is the result of values learned early in life. That's what makes our role as parents and coaches so important.

We also learn character by going through adversity. The apostle Paul said, "We know that suffering produces perseverance; perseverance, character; and character, hope" (Rom. 5:3-4). But the only thing I have seen that can radically change a person's basic character is a relationship with Jesus Christ. A person who is trying to put the teachings of Jesus Christ into practice in his life every day should begin to take on some of the character—the integrity, the patience, the truthfulness, and so on—of Christ. That's what being a Christian is all about.

The most important lesson I've learned is that God is so gracious that he accepts me—my failures, my personality quirks, my shortcomings. Believing that gives me the greatest sense of peace and security in the world.

17

Neal Jeffrey

Dwight's Insight

In 1957, my good friend James Jeffrey brought his two-year-old son, Neal, to the Fellowship of Christian Athletes summer conference in Estes Park, Colorado. From that time, I knew that Neal was destined for greatness no matter what he chose to pursue.

Neal Jeffrey was an accomplished athlete in high school and received a scholarship to Baylor University. His coach said that Neal was one of the most focused, dedicated men he had ever coached. Neal then played for the San Diego Chargers and developed a desire to use his speaking gifts in some capacity. After graduating from seminary, he realized that his speaking talent exceeded his expectations.

Motivational speakers are abundant throughout the world, but few of them have the lasting impact Neal has on an audience. His compassion and heart for the Lord are evident in all that he says and does. Neal continues to speak around the country, and he also works with Prestonwood Baptist Church.

—DLJ

Stuttering Well

When I was a kid, I had a target set up next to my garage, and as soon as I got home from school, I would practice throwing a football at that target. I would do this for hours until I could throw one hundred out of one hundred through that target. Then I would go up to my room and work on something that was maybe even more important: calling signals.

I needed to practice calling signals because I am a stutterer. I'm a really good stutterer too. But being a stutterer is really no big deal—unless you're trying to say something. Then it can be a factor. If anything, my stuttering has made my life exciting because I never know, regardless of the situation I'm in, if I'll be able to say something or not.

You can imagine the impact this had on me as a quarterback. The person in that position has to be able to talk. At the very least, he has to call plays in the huddle and yell "Hut!" at the line of scrimmage. And what if he has to call an audible once the teams are lined up? In high school, a team was allowed thirty seconds to call a play. For me, that wasn't always enough time. I'd be in the huddle, calling the play, and get stuck. I'd begin stuttering, and time would run out. The referee would throw a flag, and we'd lose five yards each time. I cost us a lot of yardage.

So my coach devised a system where he had one of the receivers stand next to me in the huddle. If I got stuck calling the play, the receiver would finish it, say the snap count, and then say, "Ready, break." My coach just said, "Neal, you be on one knee and act like you're doing something, but don't open your mouth, because it confuses everybody." So the receiver would say the play; then we would break and hustle to the line of scrimmage. The fullback who always lined up behind me would call the *hut*s for me. It was great to start a game against a new team and watch the reaction of the defense when the fullback called the *hut*s. They didn't always know where the voice was coming from.

What I want to tell you is similar to what a coach would tell you before you go out to play a game. Mostly a coach simply reminds you of things so that you'll go out and play the game of your life. I want to remind you of a few things.

Make It Count

Every game is precious, and you play the game for only so long. I played a lot of football in my life, but the fact is that I'm never going to play it again. If I was going to improve, make a difference, be the player I wanted to be, it had to be done while I was playing. My time is over. Done. I will never walk on the field again.

It's amazing how many high school athletes think, *Oh, I'll play this game forever. I've got fervor to play this game.* And then a subtle thing happens. Over time that athlete begins coasting a little. He just doesn't give everything he needs to give. He just doesn't work as hard as he ought to work, and he's kind of loafing, yet he's thinking, *One of these days I'm going to get serious about this and start doing everything. I'm going to find out how good I could be.*

The problem, though, is that he never gets there. Then before he knows it, his career is over and he's thinking, *How good could I have been if I had just given my best every day?* It would affect an athlete's life if he played every game as if this were his last, if he did every drill while thinking, *I'm not sure how long I've got, but I'm not going to waste a game.* Every practice. Every drill. *I'm going to find out how good I could become.*

This is a life lesson as well. The reason this day is such a precious thing is that you and I get to live it. The day will come when we won't get to do this anymore. You've heard the saying that any day you awake, stretch out your hand, and don't feel the side of a coffin, that's a great day. But it is true that one of these days we will not open our eyes again. So maybe we can adopt that athlete's position: *I'm not wasting a day. I'm not wasting an hour. I'm not wasting an opportunity. I'm making this day count.*

One of These Days

One of these days I'm going to kiss my wife for the last time on this earth. That's why it ought to be done today. I heard Zig Ziglar say he never left his wife without kissing her. Not a peck on the cheek either. I'm talking a long, wet kiss on the mouth. Because he knew that one day it would be his last, and he wanted each of them to go into eternity with that last kiss on their minds.

One of these days I'm going to tell my wife for the last time how precious she is to me, how my life has been enriched and blessed as the result of her love. That ought to be said today.

One of these days I'm going to play catch with my boy for the last time. He always wants to play catch, and I love playing catch. But on some days, when a lot is going on and he wants to play catch, I'm thinking that I have too much to do. But I must always remember, *Neal, you have only so long. Play catch with the boy today.*

One day you'll have your last chance to pray with your wife. How many men ever do that? Most Christian men never do. But God intended that we be intimate with our spouses, not just physically but also spiritually. Praying together binds your souls and spirits, and you become deeper and more intimate than imaginable. Pray with your wife today.

One day you'll have your last chance to share Jesus Christ with another person. We're surrounded by people who are lonely, wounded, and hopeless. They're wondering, *What is the meaning of life? I've got everything as far as money and possessions, but my life is empty.* Make this day count. We have only so long. Tell someone about Jesus today.

If you've ever been surfing, you know what it's like to sit on your board in the ocean, looking for the wave you're going to catch. You see it forming, and you say to yourself, *This is the one.* As it nears, you can feel it building around you and the undertow pulling you. You watch it curve, and you get up and hit it just right and ride it all the way to the beach. It's dynamic. It's a rush. But if you miss the wave, nothing happens. You just sit there. Today is my wave of opportunity, and I don't want to waste an hour, a minute, or a second. I want to make this day count. We have only so long. We can't waste it.

People Are Watching

When I played at Baylor, I had a lot of reasons to play well on Saturday afternoons. My family was up in the stands, the fans were cheering, and sportswriters were present. Every athlete knows that whatever he does on Saturday on the field is being captured on tape by someone in the press box. Whatever he does on Saturday will be seen again on Sunday, with commentary. He knows that whether he blows it or makes a great play, it's all being scrutinized.

The important point is simply that we are being watched.

We have to recognize that what we do every day has a powerful effect on the people around us—we are shaping lives. I've got three kids who watch their daddy, and they're probably going to go the same route as their daddy did.

My dad, James Jeffrey, was raised by his father, who was an alcoholic. His dad's side of the family drank, and his mom did too. All of them were alcoholics. When my grandfather would be gone for days at a time, sometimes weeks, my grandmother never allowed the doors to be locked, just so her husband could have an easy time getting in the house when he came home.

One day my dad's father left and never came home again. It was one of the deep hurts in my dad's life. He always hoped and prayed that he'd get to see his dad one more time. He never did.

Experts say that my dad should have been an alcoholic too. I should have been raised in the home of an alcoholic. I could have been one just as easily. But when I was at Baylor, my dad met Jesus Christ, and it changed his life forever. He started following Jesus, and everyone who was following my dad ended up following whom he was following. My brothers and their spouses all ended up going the same way, because my dad did.

How does a boy learn how to become God's man? He watches his dad be God's man. How does a boy learn how to live? He watches his dad live. How does a boy learn how to love a woman the way God wants a woman to be loved? He watches his dad love his mother. How does a boy learn how to love Jesus Christ? He watches his dad love Jesus Christ. How does a boy learn how to love God's holy Book and hide it in his heart? He watches his dad do that.

Every day matters. And every action matters. We have only so long, so let's live today as if it's our last day. Also, the tape is rolling, and someone is watching. Give today your best.

18

Carey Casey

Dwight's Insight

Carey Casey is one of the greatest expositors of the Christian faith that I have ever heard. Several years ago, I asked him to speak to a group of Christian businessmen and professionals. Many said it was one of the most powerful messages they had ever heard.

In 1988, Carey was asked to be the chaplain for the Olympic Games in South Korea. He spent several weeks reaching out to the competitors, officials, and volunteers. Carey's work with the Fellowship of Christian Athletes (FCA) in Kansas City was so powerful that the FCA asked him to be president of the FCA Foundation. Today Carey is the founder and CEO of Championship Fathering.

—DLJ

The Abundant Life

I remember a night when my dad was called a nigger. It was a very scary night when my brothers and sisters and I were in the family car, and my dad ran out of gas. He had to walk about a mile to a gas station, and when he got there, he saw several white men sitting on stools, drinking beer.

"I need some gas," my dad said.

"Nigger, we're not going to give you any gas," said one of the men.

It was in situations like this that my dad put his feet to his faith. His Christianity wasn't just in the Baptist church back home. His faith included his mind and his heart. He was able to negotiate with that man without it becoming a physical confrontation, and we got gas that night. His response set me on a course of acting in a similar way.

My dad was smart about things like race. When I was a young athlete, he got me involved in the Fellowship of Christian Athletes. He told me it was not the Fellowship of Colored Athletes but the Fellowship of Christian Athletes. When other dads were telling their kids, "Don't get on that bus, because it's white," my dad had the vision to have his children schooled cross-culturally. He saw that it was all about relationships.

With the FCA, you take a black kid from the inner city and make him roommates with a white kid from the suburbs. They start out the week thinking, *I'm rooming with a nigger* or *I'm rooming with a honky*. But they compete together, they eat together, and they hear the gospel of Jesus Christ together, and that message goes from their brains to their hearts, and their hearts get changed. Then they become new creatures, and the world around them begins to change.

Whatever color you are, God is asking, *What are you going to do with what you have?* People around the world know what a great country this is. People are trying to move here from other countries by the millions. But if we don't do something about the problems in this country, where people are truly hurting, we're going to be in trouble. Other kingdoms have fallen, and America is not exempt. We are to be stewards of this country and the world. How is Christ calling us to do that?

Relocation

We are to be in relationships with people other than those who are just like us. For me, that meant relocating. I moved from the suburbs to the inner city because I think God wanted me entering into relationships with the world around me. If you look around at our inner cities, you will see that a cancer is spreading. There is a cancer where our young people live, where I live. And when you have cancer, you have to do surgery or the cancer will spread.

Our children and grandchildren won't survive in society if it keeps going the way it is going. The bottom line is, we can't be in this life for ourselves only. We have to enter into relationships in parts of society that make us uncomfortable. This is not a problem that can be solved by throwing money at it. The surgery that is needed is invasive surgery, where we physically move to the area that needs us most.

Where I live, drug dealers are on the street corners. When I walk outside, everyone asks me for money. It's a neighborhood where conflicts are resolved with gunshots. But I moved to the inner city because I believe that we have to be there with people and that people have to see a sermon, not just hear one. My daughter asked me one Sunday morning, as we were getting dressed for church, "Daddy, are you going to be a sermon today?" That has stuck with me. When I talk to men's groups, I tell them to be strong, to run their businesses with integrity, to be smart, to stay on top of the trends. But what it really gets down to is that they must be sermons to their wives, their children, and the people they work with.

When we moved to the inner city, the biggest drug house was right next door. I saw more drugs sold out of that house than at any Walgreens. Little kids would come out of that house and ask my wife what she had on her finger.

"It's my wedding ring," she said.

"You're married to him?" they asked.

"Yes, Pastor Casey is my husband."

They hadn't seen a married couple. They hadn't seen a family.

That drug house isn't there anymore. Our church bought it and tore it down. Now we own two blocks of the street. We have gyms. We have a medical clinic that sees two thousand people a week. If you can't pay the medical fees, then you sweep the gym or pick up the paper around the neighborhood. No one loses their dignity. We have a development corporation, making it possible for people to lease a home, then purchase it.

The way things have gone through government programs is completely backward. You don't get anywhere if people are waiting around for someone to give them something without working for it. Work ethic doesn't have a color label on it. What people need is to be taught from the Word about how to be a Christian and how to work.

Some people feel that we are being dumb, living in this kind of environment, that we are putting our family in danger. Not everyone is called to do things exactly as we do. But as Dr. Martin Luther King said, "If a man has not discovered something that he will die for, he isn't fit to live."

Jesus doesn't call us to be comfortable. He calls us to be conformable to his will and to himself. For many of us, that means we have to relocate to where he can use us with the most impact. Some people who want to become missionaries don't need to leave this country. They just need to move to the city.

Redistribution

People need to get in their communities and make an economic difference. We have to bring in businesses where there are none. For years there was not one place to sit and have a nice meal in our neighborhood. So we went into business with a pizzeria. At first people said, "You can't do it. It will lose money. It will be broken into." But eventually the company agreed to take the chance. They connected their test store to our church and hired our people.

All of us are blessed to live in this country. The things it will take to make it better don't cost a lot of money. I think it will take God getting in the minds and hearts of church members so they will begin to say, "What can my church do? What can my family do? What can I do personally?" There is enough money in churches in America to do what needs to be done in our cities and to respond to what God is calling us to do.

Not too long ago, I was driving down the street when a car pulled up behind me with its lights blinking and horn blowing, as if to say, "Get out of my way." Eventually he pulled alongside me and used some sign language in my direction. The driver was white, and he was not suggesting that he loved me.

Suddenly I felt the same way I did when I played football at the University of North Carolina. My foot went down on the accelerator. Everywhere his car went, I followed him. We sped through school zones because he was trying to get away and I wouldn't let him.

Then he pulled into a gas station, and I pulled in next to him. His wife jumped out and ran inside, while I got out of my car and banged on his window.

I didn't want to say it, but the first words out of my mouth were "God bless you and I love you!"

I know for a fact that Jesus can change a person's heart. Your worst enemy can become your friend. Satan comes to steal, kill, and destroy. But Jesus comes so that we might have life and have it more abundantly (John 10:10). The abundant life, I believe, is the life that acts like Jesus, crossing boundaries and barriers and living the sermon that he preached wherever we go.

19

Tom Osborne

Dwight's Insight

At the Estes Park, Colorado, summer conference for the Fellowship of Christian Athletes, I met Tom Osborne. We kept in touch throughout his successful career as a football coach for the University of Nebraska. Everyone could see that one of the most significant aspects of Tom's personality was his character. The courage of his convictions was evident when he spoke from his heart on serious and controversial issues.

As a way to give back to Nebraska, the state that had given him so much for so many years, Tom served in the House of Representatives. Most people would have considered retiring at that point in their lives. Not Tom. He and Nancy are continuing to carry on for Jesus.

—DLJ

Living for Others

Character is in short supply in our country, in my opinion, and it's something that we all need to think about. The only thing that endures is character. At the end of the road, when everything is over in your life, it's not going to be very critical how many games you won, what kind of an athlete or coach you were, how much money you made, or what kinds of jobs you've had. The most important thing will be your character.

Discipline

The first thing I wanted the players I coached to understand was the importance of discipline. I'm not talking about the kind of discipline where parents would spank their children or take away their car keys. I'm talking about the discipline that has to do with work ethic. In coaching, we repeat, repeat, repeat, and do it right each time so that when the heat's on and the game is on the line, the team will perform correctly.

After each fall season, we have winter conditioning, spring football, and summer conditioning. Before the season starts, it is 75 percent determined, based on how well we stuck to the discipline of those off-season workouts. We don't make a lot of changes after the season begins, so that discipline is critical.

But discipline is also crucial in our spiritual lives. Without it, a good spiritual experience will last about four days and then will become only a pleasant memory. If you're in a good place spiritually right now, it's because your discipline has carried you through hard times.

Paul said in 1 Corinthians 9:25, "Everyone who competes in the games goes into strict training. They do it to get a crown that will not last, but we do it to get a crown that will last forever." Athletes prepared rigorously for the Greek games near Corinth. They went to a training camp. They didn't see their families for ten months. They worked unbelievable hours to win a wreath of pine branches that, within days, would turn brown.

Paul knew that if people worked that hard for a wreath that would last only days, it would take work to gain a wreath that would last forever. In 2 Timothy 1:7, he said, "God did not give us a spirit of timidity but one of power, love, and self-discipline" (ISV). I told this to our players just before a bowl game. In my opinion, the self-discipline comes before the power and the love. If you discipline yourself, if you pay the price spiritually, you'll begin to experience those fruits of the Spirit that will result in power and in the ability to love other people.

Perseverance

We live in a culture of the quick fix. One of the most difficult things I had to do with our players was deal with their desire for instant gratification. They wanted to be stars after eight or nine days of practice. That's just not the way life is. Nothing is that easy.

Each year, I would meet with a group of young men who were at the University of Nebraska for the first time. I would say something like this to them: "Fellows, look around the room, because, in two or three years, only about 75 percent of you will still be here. The things that will determine who's still here and who isn't won't be what you think they'll be. The single most important factor that will determine who's still here will be the level of perseverance one player has over another."

I think the same is true in a person's spiritual life. It's easy to live at a high spiritual level when you're at a retreat with great scenery and great speakers and great music. But that's only one week out of the rest of your life. Paul said that five times he was given thirty-nine lashes. Three times he was beaten with rods. Three times he was shipwrecked. He spent a day and a night in the open ocean. He was stoned and left for dead (2 Cor. 11:24–25). And remember what he did each time? He went out to the corner and started preaching again. He had great courage. And perseverance.

I have noticed that the differentiating factor between people who are successful and people who are not is how they react to failure. Every person is going to experience discouragement, disappointment, and failure, but successful people will look at failure as a temporary setback. They will say, "I'm going to get better because of this situation."

Be a Team Player

There were essentially two kinds of players who started our football program. One group would say, "I wonder if I might make the traveling squad as a freshman?" The next time I saw players like this, they were asking whether they might be all-American as freshmen. Pretty soon we got around to talking about the Heisman Trophy. These were players who wanted me to build the program around them. It doesn't work very well that way. You can't build a program around twenty freshman players. So I would get worried when all I heard was "What's in it for me? What am I going to get out of this?" Yet that is the message I think we receive from the culture over and over again.

The other group of players was the kind that was important to me. These players operated out of the question "What can I contribute? What can I do to make this team a better team?"

One year we had a receiver who was a senior from California. We were in the middle of two-a-day practices, workouts that lasted about fourteen hours a day. I was very tired one night when I heard voices down the hall. I thought everyone had gone home, so I went to the locker room. There was this receiver, standing at the blackboard. He had all ten of our freshman receivers there, going over the pass patterns with them. These players were trying to take his job away from him. He was tired and he knew the stuff cold. He could have gone home an hour earlier. But he was a guy who was interested in what he could contribute.

Jesus lived for others, as a servant. It's been said that unless a life is lived for others, it's not worth living. I believe that.

Balance

A lot of my players thought the ultimate goal was to play for the National Football League. But in the NFL, according to the players' association, the average career of a player is a little over three years. It's estimated that 78 percent of the players have gone bankrupt or are under financial stress within two years of leaving the NFL. The divorce rate within the league is between 60 and 80 percent. What happens? At age twenty-two, they become instant millionaires. They have name recognition. They have celebrity, youth, and talent. If you believe the television commercials, they have everything anyone could want. Yet so many of them come out the other end as broken people. Why?

The reason is that they are one-dimensional people. They know how to tackle. They know how to block. They know where the weight room is. But they have no spiritual depth. I never felt good about a player of ours who left our program without a spiritual commitment.

Jesus said, "Whoever wants to save their life will lose it" (Matt. 16:25). When I was young, I tried to save my life through football and being a good athlete. I was insecure and felt that if I was a good enough athlete, enough people would praise me and then I could feel good about myself.

When I couldn't play anymore, I went into coaching, and I tried to save my life through my win-loss record. You can't win enough games to please people. No matter how many wins, it's never quite enough. When I had heart surgery, I started wondering whether I had enough money in the bank. I wondered whether I could save my life through my financial resources.

Jesus never said that there was anything wrong with being a good athlete or being a good coach or wanting to win football games and make money. But he seems to have said that if we're counting on those things, we're going to be disappointed.

That's why the other half of what Jesus said is so crucial: "Whoever loses their life for me will find it" (v. 25). All that means is that Jesus must be first in our lives. There's no middle ground. We can't have it both ways. When we're willing to serve him with the talents we have, then life will take on a new dimension.

I have one goal: to honor Christ. When we lose our lives for his sake, I think we are given the strength to serve others. Our lives take on a purpose and sense of meaning that didn't exist otherwise. And when we honor and serve God, we are given a sense of stability. So many people come from disrupted families or horrendous neighborhoods. School and the workplace can be scary. But the gospel of John says, "In the beginning was the Word, and the Word was with God, and the Word was God" (1:1). Jesus always was, is, and will be. He won't change. When we base our lives on what is solid and unchangeable—something that always has been and always will be—it doesn't mean that you won't get hurt or won't lose a game or that if your family has trouble, you won't feel the pain. But you'll be supported by something powerful and stable.

There are all kinds of people who are motivated to play on Saturday afternoon. But when it's January, you have to be lifting weights. And when it's hot in July, you have to practice. Not many people are willing to do that. So, when you make your commitment, don't look back or turn away. Pay the price and follow God.

20

Rosey Grier

Dwight's Insight

A friend from Kansas City asked me to meet a friend of his, Rosey Grier. Rosey had just been hired by San Diego County to spend time reaching out to the community on a regular basis. I committed to spending a few days a month with Rosey as he made his way around the county, interacting with people in a way I had never seen. Everyone, young or old, loved Rosey.

Many people have been changed by Rosey's heart for God and his desire to make a difference for the kingdom of God with his gifts, talents, and experiences. As a singer, actor, bodyguard, football player, and celebrity, this gentle giant has constantly been used by God.

—DLJ

Turning from Darkness to Light

For a long time, my life was an exciting mix of pro football and Hollywood celebrity status. Pro football was a great adventure. Working on presidential campaigns was exhilarating. But after Bobby Kennedy was assassinated, I felt as if I were being washed ashore on a desert island. All my idealism for the future, all my hope for a change for the better, was obscured by a foggy sadness that came over me. I couldn't put my heart into anything.

What complicated things was that my personal life was out of control. Even though I was trying to help kids stay out of gangs, I wasn't doing anything to help my own life. I hadn't been able to keep my commitments in my first marriage, and my second marriage was deteriorating fast. I wanted a woman who would love and care about me, who would work with me, but not someone to whom I had to remain committed and for whom I had to be responsible.

Finally I told our little son that I was going to get a divorce.

"Dad, you shouldn't get no divorce," he said.

"You don't understand, and I can't explain it to you."

"Tell me, Dad. Tell me."

I tried, but I couldn't tell him because I was crying. I don't know whether I was crying for him or for me. Probably both. Eventually I looked at little Rosey and said, "I want to teach you something before I go. I want to teach you to pray."

I taught him the only prayer I knew, the Lord's Prayer. "He's your Father in heaven, but he's always close. He'll be with you even though I'm not. He's always taken good care of me, and he'll take care of you too."

Hitting the Bottom

When Jimmy Carter ran for president, I helped out. The Carter campaign took a great deal of my time, and the rest of it went to talking with kids in trouble, lawyers, and businesspeople. In addition, I earned my living as an actor, singer, and writer.

But none of it eased my loneliness. The joy and satisfaction I derived from my work with nonprofit groups began to disappear. I was still visiting schools and speaking, but it wasn't enough. In fact, sometimes it even seemed hopeless. I remember once lecturing kids from the street about doing right.

"Rosey," one kid asked, "what is right?"

I opened my mouth, but before I spoke, I realized I had nothing to say. "I don't know. I'm going to find out and let you know."

Before I could come up with an answer for him, he went out with a group of kids. They all got high, and for no reason, they beat him to death. I went to his funeral and wept with regret. If only I'd had an answer.

Realizing that it wasn't possible to save all the kids we worked with was a tremendous blow. That sad knowledge made my personal prison of loneliness and unhappiness close more tightly around me. I was missing something in my life. I had fame, but I wasn't happy, joyful, or content. The more I thought about it, the sorrier I felt for myself.

Throwing Out a Lifeline

I had to fly to Chicago not long after that, and the flight attendant said to me, "You're Rosey Grier, aren't you?"

I was really depressed and didn't want to talk to anyone, but I said, "Yes, I am."

She said, "I've been watching a man on television, and I think you ought to watch him."

"What does he do?" I asked.

"He teaches."

"What does he teach?"

"The Bible."

We talked for a while, and she asked for my phone number. When I got back to Los Angeles, I shut myself in my room. I understood what bitter loneliness was all about. I dropped into a pit. Then it seemed I heard a voice. *Why don't you kill yourself?*

At that moment, I understood why people kill themselves, even when they are afraid of death. Depression thrusts them to the bottom of the pit of despair and tells them they have nowhere to turn, no one to trust, no peace. Suicide seems the only alternative.

But moments after my thoughts of suicide, I thought of the time I taught little Rosey the Lord's Prayer. Then I heard myself repeating, "Our Father, who art in heaven . . ." I said the Lord's Prayer over and over, crying all the time. I held on to it as if it were a pole stretched out to a drowning man.

The next morning was Sunday, and the phone woke me up. A strange voice said, "Rosey Grier?"

"Yeah?"

"My name is Ken Ludic."

I didn't know any Ken Ludic.

"My wife told me to call you. She's an airline stewardess. She asked me to call and wake you."

I remembered her from the Chicago flight.

"Turn your television on," Ken said. "The man whose program she wants you to watch is coming on."

I got up and turned on the television. "God bless you," he said and hung up.

This is dumb, I thought. *A guy calls me up; he tells me to watch a program. I don't know what it is, and I'm sitting here like a dummy, about to watch it.*

A choir came on and sang a verse: "If they were going to convict you of being a Christian, would they have enough evidence? What does your life show?"

What did my life show? I was a desperate, lonely man.

Then the camera picked up this black man with a Bible in his hand, and he began talking about a verse and said God loved the world so much that he gave his only Son, "that whosoever believeth in him should not perish, but have everlasting life" (KJV). I picked up the Bible I hadn't read in years and tried to find the verse he'd named, John 3:16. I had no clue as to where to find the book of John. Finally I figured there must be a table of contents, and I found the page reference for the gospel according to Saint John. I turned to it and found John 3:16, and it said exactly what the man had read.

It said "everlasting life." I decided to call little Rosey. I thought he would like to hear this man also. So I called my ex-wife Margie. Our divorce had been stormy and the subject of a lot of publicity, so she was never pleased to hear from me.

"What do you want?" she asked icily.

"I really want you to let little Rosey watch this preacher on television. You can listen too."

She resisted at first, but I pleaded with her. "He's really going to want to hear this." They watched it that morning.

In spite of my Baptist pedigree, I knew nothing about God and Jesus and the Holy Spirit. I had been baptized when I was seven, and I knew some gospel songs and hymns. But as good as those things were, I hadn't made Jesus my friend. I had no relationship with God. What I did know about him was religious and not personal. Suddenly I saw how bad I needed that personal dimension.

As I listened to the preacher teach the Bible, hope began to grow in my heart. His sermon wasn't a commentary on current events and the ills of society. Instead, he commented only on the text of the Bible, with abundant applications to my daily life. I made it from week to week by watching that program.

Margie and little Rosey continued to watch every week too, and when little Rosey was with me, we watched it together. One Saturday night, Rosey said to me, "Dad, can we go over there?"

"Over where?"

"You know, that man we've been watching on television. Can we go over there?"

"Oh, Rosey, I don't want to go over there."

"Why not, Dad?"

I didn't have a good answer, so I said, "Well, sometime we'll go over there."

"Tomorrow, Dad! Let's go tomorrow!"

The next morning, little Rosey woke me up. When we got out to the car, heavy fog blanketed the area, and I was about to say, "It's too foggy to go to church." But it was as if he were reading my mind. Pretty perceptive for a seven-year-old.

"Dad, when we start somewhere, we don't turn back, do we?"

We finally made it and the place was packed. When the pastor, Fred Price, began to speak, it was as if he were addressing me in counseling chambers after listening to me spill all my troubles. Many questions I had been asking for years began to be answered that Sunday morning. I saw that it is possible to be involved in religion but not have a genuine relationship with God. I wanted to know this Jesus Dr. Price was talking about.

I became convinced that this was the missing element in my life. Through all my years I had tried to fill a hole in my life that God had put there and that only he could fill. But I had tried to fill it with people, fun, and pleasure, with good works, with money and power. I learned that John 3:16 means what it says. God gave his Son to get us back. But he never forces us to love him in return. No matter what our response, his love is steady.

At the end of the service, Dr. Price asked anyone who wanted to accept Jesus and become a new person to raise his hand. A lot of thoughts came to my mind. *You're not going to raise your hand. All these people are going to be looking at you. Don't raise your hand. You can do it later. This is your first time in this church. Why don't you wait? You can do it later.*

Up went my hand. Tears began to flow down my face, tears of relief because I had at last found a hand to hold, the hand of God. Then I saw that little Rosey had his hand up too, and tears were running down his face. Afterward, we talked with a counselor from the church, who led us in accepting Jesus.

The two of us walked out of that church that morning as new creatures in Christ.

Rebuilding a Broken Life

That was the beginning of a changed lifestyle for me. Little Rosey and I got Bibles and began going to church. Soon we could find verses without looking in the table of contents. After we had attended that church for several months, little Rosey said, "Dad, could we take Mom to church with us tomorrow?"

"I don't think so, Rosey," I said.

"But, Dad, why not?"

No matter what my feelings about Margie might be, she was his mother. If I said anything against her, little Rosey would be hurt—and rightfully so. I said, "We'll take her sometime."

"Tomorrow, Dad. Tomorrow, huh?"

I called her, figuring she would decline my invitation anyway. After all, my distaste for her company was more than matched by hers for mine.

"Little Rosey and I were thinking . . . Would you like to go to church with us?"

"Yes," she said. "I'd love to go."

"You would? Well, we have to leave early."

"I don't mind," she replied sweetly. "What time do you want me to be ready?"

I didn't know what to make of it. We found seats near the front, and little Rosey sat between us. At the end of the service, Margie shocked me again. She raised her hand and went up for counseling. She accepted Jesus and began going to church with us every Sunday.

Several months later, I began to date my ex-wife. For the first time, I was dating a woman just for the pleasure of her company, without designs or ulterior motives. We had fun and enjoyed going places together. We laughed and had things to talk about. Before the divorce, we had been together five years, but it had never been like this.

After a while, I asked her why she had so readily accepted my invitation to church when I had been so sure she would turn me down.

"I never saw anyone change the way you did in the months after you started watching Fred Price on television," she said. "And you only got better when you started going down there in person. I wanted to know more about anything that made such a dramatic and wonderful change in you. It had to be real. By the time you called, I was eager to go."

For the first time, I knew how it felt to be in love, because I was falling in love with Margie.

After we dated for about two years, Margie and I decided that we were ready to give marriage a serious try. This time, each of us had a foundation in our lives—Jesus Christ, who gave us assurance that we could succeed in him in spite of our former failure.

Most of my motivational speaking engagements were canceled after I began talking about my new life in Christ, but I was able to speak to many Christian groups and begin a new organization in Los Angeles where young people were able to learn the Bible and a trade.

When I finally called on God to help me, he took the broken pieces of my life and made me whole. Then he took the broken pieces of my family and made it whole. Those are miracles of restoration and reconciliation that point us to God as the authentic source of supply for all our needs.

I turned from darkness to light, from Satan's power to God's. And through faith, my sins were forgiven and I received my place among God's chosen people. And now I serve God by helping others experience the same. That is what the church is supposed to be doing—not forcing everyone to think alike but showing God's love to everyone.

The answer to wickedness lies not in the halls of Congress nor in the corridors of the White House. It sits, instead, atop a hill called Golgotha, and it stands at the entrance of an empty tomb.

21

Bill Kennedy

Dwight's Insight

Tim LaHaye asked me to do him a personal favor and spend about an hour with a friend of his who had moved to San Diego. That time with Bill Kennedy started one of the most incredible relationships I have ever had.

One day Bill and I were having lunch, and his fifteen-year-old son was with us. Bill told me that charges had been filed against him for something he had not been involved in. The longer he talked, the more unbelievable the story sounded. His son cried, and I realized that this was all too real.

During the trial, I learned to appreciate Bill's heart and his resolve to not admit to committing crimes that he did not commit. Bill was sentenced to a twenty-year term and was sent to a federal penitentiary. He was released after serving seventeen years.

—DLJ

The Truth Will Set You Free

When I accepted Christ, I was under the impression that if I just behaved and didn't step out of line, then everything would come up roses. But God has allowed me to see him in ways I never imagined possible.

Since we can't understand God, we create a god that we can understand. I created one out of silver and gold and carried it around with me everywhere I went. In my god's eyes, I was doing very well.

By the time I was thirty, I had graduated from college with a degree in geology, was married with three children, and was active in my church and in local politics. The value of precious metals began to rise during that time, and I was fairly successful in buying and selling them. Friends started asking for my help in buying them, so pretty soon I had a company that was selling millions of dollars in precious metals.

As I look back, it seems that I had more courage than brains. My marketing powers were greater than my business sense, and I didn't have the wisdom to hire people with the business sense. I didn't really intend for the business to grow as fast as it did. In one year, it grew by more than $40 million. An accountant looked at my company and said that our marketing was blue chip but our back office was in the Stone Age.

One of my mentors at the time told me that if I didn't keep God first, I wouldn't have any peace. That was a warning I didn't heed.

Falling from on High

Successful businesses are stressful. As things got busier and more stressful, I stopped spending time with other men and leading them to

Christ. It used to be one of my priorities, but I became too busy being successful.

Within the next four years, our sales grew, and my company was selling 25 percent of the world's investment supply of platinum. As the metals business boomed, I finally hired a manager who pointed out several flaws in our practices. His plan prompted some cutbacks, which led to some employees stealing our company's mailing list. Anyone in sales knows that the mailing list is a chief asset of any business. These former employees started competing companies, and our business went into a panic. Eventually the company went into Chapter 11 bankruptcy protection so that we could reorganize.

During my company's reorganization, my stress levels were off the chart. It was so bad that my wife finally confronted me about my temper. Debbie insisted on my getting counseling, and I finally agreed to it because I thought it would save my marriage. I called Tim LaHaye, and he agreed to counsel us.

Tim introduced me to the Holy Spirit. Tim shared that he had had similar issues and that God had delivered him from his spirit of anger. God delivered me that day. I learned to go to the Holy Spirit when I began to boil.

Chapter 11 seemed like the best option for my company because I was determined to fully pay back all our creditors. I worked out a plan and went to court to show I could pay out $18 million over ten years. The creditors and the court approved the plan, and I was relieved. I was being investigated during this time to see whether I had done anything illegal, but my lawyers assured me that I wouldn't be indicted for anything as long as I kept paying back the creditors.

As a way to start paying back my creditors, I signed a contract with the government of Kuwait just after they were invaded by Iraq. I was a registered foreign agent for them. I wanted to make sure I wasn't doing anything illegal, so I hired a lawyer with a business background whom I had met when he was a clerk during my company's bankruptcy proceedings. I was too naive to see his ulterior motives and pay attention to the political undercurrents in the US about the first Iraq war.

The *Wall Street Journal* did a story on my lobbying efforts on behalf of Kuwait, saying that I was trying to get votes in the Senate to authorize going to war. Federal prosecutors began investigating me without my knowledge.

During this time, God began bringing some strong believers into my life to disciple me. Through prayer and Bible study, I began to develop a heart for those who are lost. Driving home from a study from the book of John, I prayed that God would use me to reach those who didn't know him.

Two months later, there was a banging on my front door so loud that I thought someone was trying to break in. Federal agents had surrounded the house and had an arrest warrant for me, charging me with fraud. They handcuffed me and took me to a detention center for the night. One of my bunkmates was a Latino man who didn't speak English. But he was weeping and trying to read his Spanish-language Bible. I don't know Spanish, but I was able to find the Psalms for him, and he calmed down immediately.

Twenty-three of my former employees were also arrested that day and charged with fraud. I couldn't believe the indictment because none of it was true. During my initial hearing, the prosecutor claimed that I was an escape risk and that I had started the Persian Gulf War. The magistrate laughed and let me out on bail. Tim LaHaye and two others put their property up for collateral.

Having put most of my earnings back into the company so I could pay back creditors, I couldn't afford another attorney, so the court appointed one. It seemed that the prosecutors' case was flimsy, and my attorney assured me that I would be found innocent. All the others were acquitted, or their cases had been dismissed. But I was found guilty of money laundering and sentenced to twenty years in prison, though I never did anything of the sort.

In Prison with God

The first thing I did in prison was begin to memorize the first eleven verses of the book of James. I was determined not to let my feelings get the best of me. My wife was far away and had to go back to work after twenty-three years of being home raising our kids.

Tim insisted that I call him regularly, and he put me on a Scripture reading regimen. Through that, God began revealing sin to me. I became convicted about something in my own heart daily. At the same time, inmates began approaching me because they wanted to talk about God. I never imagined that God could use me in these men's lives. He taught me that my helping them would relieve me of my own pain.

From the beginning of my time in prison, I tried to stay busy being a witness for Christ. An elderly man came into jail one day, and no one wanted him as a cellmate, so I asked to take him in. It turned out he was a former member of the church I belonged to. He had lost his ranch to the federal government and had been filing illegal liens. He was obsessed with rebuilding his empire—it was all he could talk about.

During my time with him, I sensed God saying, *Thirty years from now, what will matter is not what you achieve but who you touched for my sake.* It dawned on me that previously I had been a nominal Christian at best. I attended church three times a week, gave more than our tithe, and helped people financially. But my real love wasn't God; it was trying to influence the direction of this country toward more conservative ideals. I loved my goals more than I loved God.

This is when God brought me to the book of Job. I began to see who God is and who I wasn't. I wasn't the lord of my life. Through Philippians 2:14, he taught me to watch out for my grumbling. In 1 Thessalonians 5:18, he showed me that I needed to give thanks in all things. One day, after listening to me gripe on the phone for fifteen minutes, Tim LaHaye told me to read five psalms and count off ten things I was grateful for. I hated that advice, but I knew he was right. Scripture showed me that a lack of gratitude is sin. Giving thanks relieved my depression. All my crutches were gone. And it seemed that God had me right where he wanted me. But occasionally it seemed that God had gone to sleep and simply had forgotten me.

Many days I didn't know how I would make it. Prison is so full of hate, expletives, and anger, and no encouraging word is ever spoken. Friendships are difficult to develop, especially for Christians. The first two years, I was housed with many violent men who mocked and threatened me. After a year or so, though, several told me that they had given their lives to Christ. They were afraid to tell anyone for fear of intimidation by those who were big, tough guys on the outside but little boys on the inside.

After I had been in jail for a month, the prosecutors in my case offered to substantially reduce my sentence. I appeared in the prosecutor's office in leg-irons and handcuffs, and the prosecutor told me that I could get out of prison much sooner if I would tell a lie about my lawyer. But the prosecutor was shocked when I declined his offer.

On the Track at Lompoc

I was transferred to the federal correctional facility in Lompoc, California. This was where I had the experience that Job had in chapter 40. This was where God brought me down to my very core, showing me who I really was. I asked him to reveal my sinful heart. I asked him to show me who he really is. It seemed that God had been only a concept until then. I told him that I wanted to be done with hanging on to myself or my sin. I told God that all I wanted in return was to wake up in the morning with joy. Waking up in prison is like waking up in hell. It is eternal torment.

The Bible told me that God loved me, but I wanted to experience that love. I wanted more than words on a page, even though they were his words. So, every morning, I walked around the prison track, praying over Scriptures and memorizing them. It still seemed that something was missing, something that kept me from intimacy with God. The only love I had really experienced was from my wife. I wanted the love that I read about in Scripture.

In the middle of one day, God broke through to my heart and I sensed him saying, *Bill, I love you so very much. Never doubt it for a moment.* I wept with joy all afternoon. Then God showed me my self-centeredness in my marriage. I had been so focused on myself that I didn't see Debbie's pain. In obsessing about my case, I put a lot of pressure on her, lecturing her on what she should be doing to help me. I wasn't ministering to her. But on that track in Lompoc, I changed. During the next visit, I told our children that their mother was a much better Christian than me because she exemplified the life of Christ.

Tim LaHaye and others sent me phone money so I could call Debbie every night. I also tried to prepare a devotional for our son. One night, just before Christmas, my wife was crying when I called. She had needed emergency dental surgery, which wiped out our bank account.

We prayed on the phone, and within two days, Dwight Johnson and members of our church brought over a check that more than covered the bill. This happened several times when we were at the very last dollar. Our Sunday school class supported us. Even my eighth-grade science teacher, James Dobson, sent my wife a check during an emergency. We never told anyone about our emergencies. These provisions came not from any solicitation on our part but from the Holy Spirit prompting these people's hearts.

I saw that God was more interested in our character than in our comfort. When we were totally dependent on him, he provided more than we needed. During one conversation with our Sunday school teacher, I began complaining about the unfairness of our plight.

"Bill, who are you ministering to?" he asked.

No one, I thought. It was all about me. But it's not about us, is it? It's about God and letting him use us in the lives of others. As I continued to walk the Lompoc track, God began to show me how to relate to the men in that prison. The characters in prison are like the characters in the bar scene in *Star Wars*. It was like they were all from a primitive tribe, and they frequently upset me. But I sensed God saying, *Bill, I love these men. I don't love what they do, but I love them. Try to look at them through my eyes.*

God gave me the worst bunkmate in all of Lompoc. But God used him to lead another inmate to Christ. My bunkmate refused to speak to me as we lived in this six-foot-by-nine-foot cube. He was rude to me, and I responded in kind. This went on for months. But I sensed God telling me to love him, so for every mean thing he did, I showed him kindness. Eight men in nearby cells watched this. Eventually one of them, a man from Colombia who hadn't spoken to me in two years, asked me whether I had a Bible he could read. He accepted Christ soon after.

I am often tempted to ask what might have been, but that's a trap. All of us have regrets. I know God is good, and I am privileged to witness his redemptive work in me and others. The reason I don't have regrets is that I have come to know God the way Job knew him. I am thankful for

Job and for the apostle Paul because their stories encourage me. Maybe my story will help someone else who is going through troubling times.

We're all in some kind of prison, figurative or literal. My prayer is that God will use your prison experience—as he did for Job, Paul, and me—to show his true nature so that you might do more than know about him. He wants us to know him.

22

Christopher Williams

Dwight's Insight

Christopher Williams is truly one of a kind. I met him years ago at a conservative meeting of like-minded people and found him to be a fascinating person. We have had many wonderful discussions. I have found many lawyers to be so opinionated that their perspectives tend to be biased. Christopher, on the other hand, is able to understand other people's feelings and deal with them accordingly. He taught me to be less biased and more interested in the overall discussion than I used to be, and at my age, that is a blessing.

—DLJ

Second Chances

In the late 1960s, my uncle died of an asthma attack because a Virginia hospital wouldn't treat him because of his race. The three-hour ride to another hospital eventually killed him. Segregation had a significant impact on me, but I didn't allow this evil to make me embittered. Instead, I used the anger this injustice provoked to fuel my ambition to live well—in a way that was not only honoring to God but also healing for my family.

Strong Roots

My parents were loving but very strict. There were seven boys in the family. Each sibling was responsible for the brothers who were younger than he was. If the youngest one did something, then we all had to be disciplined. If the oldest did something, the rest of us just laughed.

One of the most influential figures in my life was my father. As an effective and no-nonsense preacher, he was well respected, not only in his church but also in the community. My dad's church was very conservative, both in its theology and in its culture.

Dad constantly reminded us that to be a leader means to be a servant and that there is no greater honor than to serve with your abilities. He never had an education past the eighth grade. He went to a training school, but the men of color weren't allowed to do anything but get a certificate to go to trade school. So he began working for a construction company that built hotels in Virginia Beach. He never made a salary being a pastor; he always had to keep his hands dirty to put food on the table.

My mother ran a business and taught us to be entrepreneurs. But her priority was always her faith. My grandmother was also very humble. She worked her entire life as a maid, putting on a white uniform every day and working in mansions. She never even stole so much as an ink pen. She never used profanity. She defined sainthood. But she did that job because that was all that was available.

My father would always say to my mother, "We raised them right, so they will do the right thing." Once, he told me I had appeared in one of his dreams. I was on a precipice, and God was holding out his hand to me. That's all he said—no interpretation.

I have a bit of an independent streak. When my father and I were working construction, he would call me "boy" and I would tell him where to go. So I went and got my own job. I started washing dishes for a quarter an hour. Years later, my father told me that I had gotten too wrapped up in the excess of the world, and I took that to heart. Pastors have a lot of sayings. My father had a lot of them. I put together a book of the ones I could remember. Now I'm passing those teachings along to my grandchildren.

My brothers and I deeply respected our father. If he had ended up in the military, he would have been a general. He had been the top ROTC cadet in the country. He found out later he had a hole in his heart and couldn't serve in the military. Things change just like that. But if you're a smart person, you can do something else.

My mother says that even though my dad and I were diametrically opposed, we were still very much alike. He raised us to put God first, then family. He instilled great dreams in us: one of us would be an architect, another a CPA, another a doctor, and another a lawyer. When I said I was going to be a doctor, he said, "No, your cousin is going to be the doctor."

When my father was only nineteen, the local newspaper did an article about his construction abilities because he was extraordinary. But then companies would tell him that he couldn't have a job because they all required a high school diploma and all he had was a training certificate. This represented the worst of institutionalized racism.

In the 1950s, schools began to integrate. They had a federal order to do it, and they weren't too happy about it. But we still had the option to stay in colored schools. I decided to integrate because I wanted to choose from the best options available to me. In high school I was always the only colored student in the advanced classes. My cousin had gone to that high school the year before I did, but she could pass as Caucasian because of her light skin. My little brother ran track and became a star at the school. We were all just breaking down barriers.

I wandered a bit in college, starting out as a chemistry major and then heading toward med school. That turned into a chemical engineering major because I wanted to fly and engineers had an easier time getting those jobs. But the need for corrective lenses kept me out of the cockpit, so I switched to economics. During this time of exploration, I realized that none of these fields represented my true calling—the law. Eventually I became one of the most influential attorneys on the East Coast.

On Race and Color

Color reinforces the stereotypical judgments we make about people. When I joined the US Navy, they asked me to indicate my race on the application. I put down *human*. When I arrived for training, someone had crossed it off and put down *negroid*. I let them know, in no uncertain terms, "You don't know who I am." So I kept putting down *human* on the race line.

These days, when asked about my race, I will pick an ancestor and identify with him or her. Sometimes I put down Caucasian because I am one-eighth white. My children will often do the same thing. One of my daughters has very fair skin, but her DNA test reveals all kinds of ethnic blood. She could pass as Caucasian or Native American or African American—and all would be true. The idea that anyone would stereotype my kids based on their looks infuriates me—so I confront it whenever that kind of bias rears its ugly head.

On Career

I was the first attorney of color in Virginia Beach. I attended the University of Virginia, considered by many to be part of the Ivy League of the South. I worked hard and caught a few breaks, but it's been a long, hard road.

On the bar exam application back then, you had to put down your race. As always, I put down *human*. Then the Supreme Court said that you could no longer ask for race in the application. The military still did but not the state bar. So the next year in Virginia, they started asking for a picture.

I've spoken about this around the country. It didn't matter how smart I was. They didn't want me. There were more than four hundred of us in the class, and only about eighteen were colored.

After law school, I was offered a judgeship. I would have been the youngest judge in the history of this state. But I got a call that said I shouldn't run for any kind of office because I'd be sticking my neck out and making myself a target.

My dad was a Republican, and so was my grandfather, but neither of my grandfathers voted. You would get lynched if you voted.

At one point, a law firm said that I should take all the minority cases in their state from them. I didn't like that, so I said no. In San Diego I landed some fortunate cases where I went head to head with the first firm and whipped them. Those victories gave me a big break. That's when I started doing bond work, which was a very specialized area, and very few people could do it, even across the country. My specialty became corporate financing.

I represented a lot of sports figures too. We also did movie financing. I was involved in setting up the Minority Business Enterprise (MBE), which now provides certification for qualified entrepreneurs. I set up an e-commerce company through them and then began to hire through the MBE.

I moved to New York City, where one of my connections promised multiple clients from New York to LA, and he came through. We had a good relationship and could talk about anything. He was Jewish, a little more liberal than most, and I just kept sharing the gospel with him. He was the one who gave me a kick start. From that opening, we got into major-league corporate finance, banking, real estate, and a lot of business in California.

The reason I kept getting hired was that I was trusted and had a reputation for strong ethics. Keeping high standards opened all kinds of doors. Sometimes clients would describe me as "the Christian lawyer," and I loved that. In my line of work, I've been able to able to share the gospel with Muslims, Hindus, atheists, and agnostics. You are always making a statement for Christ.

On Second Chances

In my early years, I loved boxing, but fighting for sport took a toll on me. I had to have several boxing-related surgeries to address the impact on my eyes. On top of color blindness, the recovery process has taken its toll over the years. Complications from being in a coma and scarring on my retinas is beginning to diminish my ability to see.

I've had three heart attacks, two in one year. At the time of the first one, my bond practice was very stressful. We had won a huge settlement against a corporation, but then my heart took a hit. I thought I was Superman, but the *S* on my chest just stood for "stupid." I had bypass surgery, rested for thirty days, and then had another heart attack. The first was serious, but the second was massive. The doctor called it a widow-maker. My cardiologist couldn't believe I was still alive. Then, within a year, I had a stroke. For a short time, I was using a wheelchair and then a walker.

After the second heart attack, my kids were all there when I woke up from surgery. I quit my law practice on the spot. I quit just about everything and decided to rest and wait on the Lord. God gave me a second chance, and I wasn't going to blow it.

Eventually I began rehab and stuck with it for three and a half years (some of that was going through speech therapy and then learning to walk again). Then I had my third heart attack in 2013. Through stem cell treatment, parts of my heart have begun to regenerate. I attribute the fact that I'm still around to being a bona fide miracle.

I did yoga, got into martial arts, became a vegetarian. I studied all the world religions. I learned about all the Hindu gods and the Babylonian gods. Confucius, Tao—all of that. All that exposure only brought me closer to Jesus Christ. He's the only one who makes any sense.

I've looked death in the eye multiple times, and I can't believe I'm still alive. All of it has just pushed me to be a better husband, father, and grandfather. Two of my girls are missionaries. The other two went to Christian schools and married chaplains.

I want to always stay cognizant of all the God moments in my life. The challenge these days is that I'm told not to mention Jesus Christ at schools where I'm asked to speak. I do anyway. They want me to talk about who is most influential in your life. It's Jesus Christ, hands down. I talk about how Jesus changed my life.

I've been broke three times in my life, and I made it back up. I've lost a little less than $5 million in the last couple of years. The point is that you have to keep going. I'm blessed. My first year in law practice, I made eight cents profit—eight pennies. I kept them in a jar.

I eventually made it to New York City with an office on the sixteenth floor of a beautiful building. It had to be nice to draw in a certain type of clientele. I hired a decorator to do what needed to be done, because you have clients who have certain expectations and you need to create an ambience for them. But that's what they are trapped in. I didn't want to be trapped in that. Even so, the overhead was tremendous, and I had fifteen lawyers and forty other people on staff. That's a lot of stress. That's what causes heart attacks.

Life is like a droplet of water on the end of a piece of thread. Oh, how fragile it is. I've learned that even great loss is like a droplet of water. It means nothing in life, so I just let it go. I only look for God moments with people, because that's the only thing that's going to matter in heaven. That means living so that others would have an opportunity to see Christ in my life and want to experience that.

One guy said he watched me for thirty years before he committed his life to Christ—he needed to know it was real in at least one person's life. You just never know what sort of impact you're having.

My mother would constantly remind us to look with the eyes of Jesus. If I'm looking through the eyes of Christ, I'm not going to be able to judge another person's heart or motives. Jesus always held out his hand. He never pointed a finger at those who were seeking him. Yes, he had a few strong words for the religious leaders who were putting burdens on people that they themselves could never bear. But he always had compassion on the penitent.

You're always going to deal with evil until Christ comes back. We're supposed to reflect Christ through the power of the Holy Spirit. If people see the Holy Spirit in you, then they're going to want to know more about that. Christ will fight that battle.

23

Tim Philibosian

Dwight's Insight

When my wife and I met Tim and Lyn Philibosian, we saw they loved the Lord, loved life, and loved each other very much. Tim had the largest Christian law practice in Colorado; then he went back to school to get his divinity degree and for years was recognized by many as the premier authority on the New Age movement.

After Tim sold his law practice, he joined me in my company, Sturgeon Systems, as our in-house legal counsel. He helped me evaluate many investment opportunities and business relationships as well.

Tim and his family have suffered more medical hardships and setbacks than any other family I have known. Despite these circumstances, Tim and Lyn have remained strong in the faith, resolved to live like Christ.

—DLJ

Be That Man

While driving my car one day, I was listening to a message by Walter Martin, the founder of the Christian Research Institute. He was saying that men were not seeking truth and were instead turning to myths, to ear-tickling teachers who said what they wanted to hear. He emphasized that what was needed were men who were willing to take a stand, men who were willing to refute false teachers, men who were willing to endure hardship, to pay the price. Then he shouted, "Who will be that man?"

I practically jumped out of the car, thrusting my fist through the roof of that 1971 Mercury Capri (fortunately, the sunroof was open) as I shouted, "I will be that man!" Little did I realize the significant price that would be extracted from me for the words I spoke that night.

Following God's Leading

After deciding to "be that man," I worked with the prayer breakfast movement in Washington, DC, meeting with individuals, attending prison Bible studies, and exploring ministry and educational alternatives. I made two significant decisions: first, to get married; and second, to attend seminary.

I had been dating Lyn Kirby, a woman who shared my interest in Christian service. Realizing I didn't want to face life without her, I proposed to Lyn, and two weeks later, we were married. Two days after that, we boarded a plane for Vancouver, British Columbia. After one semester at Regent College, we moved to Colorado, where I completed my master of divinity at Denver Seminary.

It had always been my intention to resume my legal career, so I accepted an offer from a Christian lawyer to join his practice. But when I became involved in trying to keep New Age curriculum out of the local schools, I approached my senior partner to tell him I was going to take a six-month leave of absence. That was in April 1983. I never returned to the full-time practice of law.

I formed my own nonprofit organization, Rivendell, in 1987. Our desire was to stand against those elements of society that sought to promote religious beliefs in conflict with Christianity. We conducted seminars throughout the nation on topics such as Islam, Satanism, witchcraft, the New Age movement, and Mormonism. We provided workshops and training sessions on the right to life, creation/evolution, reincarnation, psychics, apologetics, and persuasion skills.

In late February 1992, I was scheduled to speak at the opening session of a men's conference in Beaver Creek, Colorado. I drove eagerly toward the mountains, even though snow had started to fall. But the driver ahead of me apparently was focused on something else. His car spun out of control, slid across the highway, and came to a thudding stop against a guardrail. Without thinking, I stopped alongside the highway and ran back to render assistance. I helped the driver out of the car, and we started to assess the damage to the front end.

That's all I remember.

Run with the Horses

I was told a driver in a pickup truck was accelerating too quickly for the conditions, spun out of control, and hit the wrecked car, which then hit me. Later, a neurologist told me I was hit by a force equal to that of Reggie Jackson taking a home-run cut at a fastball.

I was in a coma for several days. My vision was seriously affected; the most obvious symptom was double vision, which required that I wear an eye patch. The severe blow to my forehead damaged my olfactory nerves so that I lost my sense of smell and therefore had a difficult time distinguishing any taste. My ability to walk was also seriously affected. I had terrible headaches and required enormous amounts of sleep. My memory was sketchy; my ability to speak, impaired.

Doubts filled my mind. How could I prepare my talks? How could I plan seminars? Would I be able to write or speak effectively again? *God, why would you allow this? All I was trying to do was serve you. Why would you allow this to happen?*

My questions were from the depths of my heart. I was reminded of Jeremiah's pleading in Jeremiah 12: "God, I have a case against you. You've asked me to represent you, to speak. I've done that, and all I've received in return is sarcasm, taunts, prison, the stocks, even death threats. God, is this what you want? Why do you allow wickedness to prosper? Why do you do things this way?"

God's response to Jeremiah is classic: "Jeremiah, what are you whining about? I haven't asked you to do any more than I've asked of so many others. I'm training you for the battles that lie ahead. If you can't walk with the footmen, how will you ever learn to run with the horses? And that's where I want you, Jeremiah—running with the horses. Don't quit; don't be content simply to get by. Run with the horses."

That was God's message to me as well.

Physical Challenges

Almost exactly one year after the car accident, I was preparing for another Beaver Creek speaking engagement. The men had asked me to come back to report on the accident and share what God had been doing in my life.

A few days before I was to leave for the mountains, I developed pink eye. The doctor prescribed medication that caused excruciating pain when I put it in my eyes. My wife called the nurse, who said, "Yes, it can be painful. Just tell him to tolerate it." Refusing to believe it should hurt like this, I read the label carefully and found that the medication I had been given was mistakenly dispensed—it wasn't meant to be put in the eyes.

An ophthalmologist spent the next several hours rinsing and observing my eyes. When he released me, he said that I should be okay but that my eyes would be extremely sensitive for the next week or so and that I couldn't drive.

The car accident had almost killed me. My vision was significantly affected. I couldn't smell, so my taste was affected. The medication mistake nearly cost me my sight. When would this end? Still, I wanted to "be that man" and "run with the horses." What strategy would Satan try next in his effort to destroy me? He assaulted my family.

I used to say that there were two reserved parking zones at the emergency room: ambulance parking and "the Philibosian zone." It seemed the staff knew us all by name. "Ah, it is the Philibosians. Your regular room?"

Within the next few months, my older son, JT, fell and broke his arm. He had an operation to set it, and that operation had to be repeated six months later because it wasn't done properly the first time. After that, JT was at a youth camp when he was misdiagnosed as having the flu. It turned out he had appendicitis. Several days later, when he finally was taken to a hospital for an emergency operation, the surgeon told us he had been within hours of dying. Then JT's temperature wouldn't go down. He had to have another operation, his fourth in less than two years.

My younger son, Mark, ran into a basketball pole, which cut his face seriously. Numerous stitches were required. Then, when he was at church, one of the youth staff took a swing with a broomstick at a piñata. He missed the stick and crushed Mark's cheekbone, nearly putting out his eye.

My daughter, Joylyn, had to be taken to the emergency room when she began choking on a fish bone that required professional expertise to remove.

Physical challenges never seemed to relent. The worst—at least since the car accident—occurred in July 1995 when we were staying near Lake Dillon, Colorado, for a family vacation. Immediately before our return to Denver, we took a family photo of all of us on our mountain bikes. From our condo to the photo spot was only a block or two, but we decided to take the long way back.

For me, it turned out to be a very long way back. I missed a turn and fell off a cliff, hurtling over huge boulders and experiencing a sensation I had never before felt. I was taken up the cliff on a backboard with cables. After a short stay in a medical center, a helicopter flew me to the emergency room at Denver General Hospital. Diagnosis: A broken back. Fractured vertebrae.

After my release, I had to stay in a hospital bed for five months. The bed wouldn't fit in our bedroom, so I was confined to our living room.

Since my back was broken, I had to wear an uncomfortable brace or lie flat. In order to turn, which I had to do every few hours, I had a bell that I rang, waking Lyn so that she could assist.

God, why are you doing this? All I've wanted to do is serve you. I've given you everything. What more do you want from me?

His answer: silence.

"Be that man!" I told myself. "Run with the horses!"

More Attacks

It was during my recuperation that a church in Santa Barbara, California, asked me to be its senior pastor. I had spoken at the church and knew a number of its people. Events worked together to the point where I agreed to accept the position.

My determination was to "be that man" despite Satan's many attempts to sidetrack me. There were times of disappointment, heartache, and frustration, but I never gave up, and I never went back. I never doubted God, although at times I sure thought he could have worked things out a little differently.

Now Satan's strategy was to attack me emotionally and spiritually, challenging my self-confidence, leadership, and abilities—through critics within my own church. This was the most devastating attack of all.

When I planned the first church-wide fundraising effort to modernize our facilities and construct a new building, a surreptitious countereffort was planned. While our campaign was successful, the seeds of future provocation were sown.

Some in the church began to question my decisions, undermine my authority, and belittle my messages. Rumor, innuendo, and accusations spread throughout the church. Divisions were formed; disunity became common. Gossip became acceptable behavior.

Finally I was at the breaking point. I asked myself, *Will you continue to live the faith you have been speaking of all these years?* While I refused to back down from my commitment to "be that man," I realized that God was leading me to a new battlefield. On July 31, 2005, after years of serving the church in Santa Barbara, I resigned.

Never Give Up

To give up, to doubt, to quit when circumstances seem to be going against us would deprive us of our opportunity to let God use us for his glory, to work through us in a way that can be clearly seen as God's accomplishment and not ours.

Who knows what God will do in and through a man devoted to him? All I know is that I want to be ready.

24

Josh McDowell

Dwight's Insight

When I met Josh McDowell, he was traveling around the world, speaking to thousands of people. He had just finished his book More Than a Carpenter, *and its success seemed to be almost instantaneous.*

It is so difficult for most of us parents to effectively communicate with our kids without them thinking that we are preaching. As more people heard Josh and realized the gifts God had given him to speak to young people, more and more opportunities presented themselves. Over the past sixty years, he has spoken to more than twenty-five million people. It is a blessing to know a man like Josh who is able to communicate God's unconditional love so sincerely.

—DLJ

Replacing Restlessness with Love

As a teenager, I wanted to be happy. I wanted to be one of the happiest individuals in the entire world. I also wanted meaning in life. I wanted answers to questions such as, Who am I? Why am I here? Where am I going?

More than that, I wanted to be free. Freedom to me is not going out and doing what you want to do. Anyone can do that, and lots of people are doing it. Freedom is having the power to do what you know you ought to do. Most people know what they ought to do, but they don't have the power to do it. They're in bondage.

So I started looking for answers. It seemed that almost everyone was into some sort of religion, so I did the obvious thing and took off for church. I must have found the wrong church, though. Some of you know what I'm talking about: I felt worse inside the church than I did outside.

I began to wonder whether prestige was the answer. Being a leader, accepting some cause, giving yourself to it, and being known for it might do it, I thought. So I ran for freshman class president and got elected. It was great, but it wore off like everything else I had tried. I would wake up Monday morning, and my attitude was "Well, here goes another five days." I endured Monday through Friday. Happiness revolved around the weekend. Then the vicious cycle began all over again.

Meaning and Purpose

At my university I noticed a group of eight students and two faculty members. They seemed to know what they believed and why they believed. I like to be around people like that. I don't care if they don't agree with me. Some of my closest friends are opposed to some things I believe, but I admire a man or woman with conviction.

The people in this small group didn't just talk about love. They got involved. They seemed to be riding above the circumstances of university life. One important thing I noticed was that they seemed to have a happiness not dependent on circumstances. They had something I didn't have. So I decided to make friends with these intriguing people.

Two weeks after that decision, we were all sitting around a table in the student union. The conversation started to get around to God. I looked over at one of the students, a good-looking woman, and I leaned back in my chair because I didn't want the others to think I was interested. I said, "Why are your lives so different from the other students'?"

She looked me straight in the eye and said two words I never thought I'd hear as part of a solution at a university: "Jesus Christ."

I said, "I'm fed up with religion. I'm fed up with the church. I'm fed up with the Bible."

She shot back, "I didn't say 'religion.' I said 'Jesus Christ.'" She pointed out something I'd never known before. Christianity is not a religion. Religion is humans trying to work their way to God through good works. Christianity is God coming to men and women through Jesus Christ, offering them a relationship with himself.

My new friends challenged me intellectually to examine the claims that Jesus Christ is God's Son, that he lived among real men and women and died on the cross for the sins of mankind, that he was buried and arose three days later and could change a person's life today.

I thought this was a farce. In fact, I thought most Christians were walking idiots. I imagined that if a Christian had a brain cell, it would die of loneliness. But these people challenged me over and over. Finally I accepted their challenge, but I did it out of pride, to refute them. I didn't know there were facts. I didn't know there was evidence that a person could evaluate. Eventually I concluded that Jesus Christ must have been who he claimed to be.

A Change of Heart

At that time, though, I had quite a problem. My mind told me all this was true, but my will was pulling me in another direction. I discovered that becoming a Christian was rather ego shattering. Jesus Christ made a direct challenge to my will, urging me to trust him.

If you've ever been around happy people when you're miserable, you understand how they can bug you. Every time I was around those enthusiastic Christians, the conflict would begin. They would be so happy and I would be so miserable that I'd literally get up and run right out of the room. It came to the point where I'd go to bed at ten at night and I wouldn't get to sleep until four in the morning. I knew I had to get it off my mind before I went out of my mind. I was always open-minded but not so open-minded that my brains would fall out.

But since I was open-minded, during my second year at the university, I became a Christian.

Somebody asked me, "How do you know?" I said, "It changed my life." That night, I prayed four things. First, I said, "Lord Jesus, thank you for dying on the cross for me." Second, I said, "I confess those things in my life that aren't pleasing to you and ask you to forgive me and cleanse me." Third, I said, "Right now, in the best way I know how, I open the door of my heart and life and trust you as my Savior and Lord. Take over the control of my life. Change me from the inside out. Make me the type of person you created me to be." The last thing I prayed was "Thank you for coming into my life by faith."

I'm sure you've heard various religious people talking about their "bolt of lightning." Well, after I prayed, nothing happened. I mean, nothing. And I still haven't sprouted wings. In fact, after I made that decision, I felt worse. *Oh no. What'd you get sucked into now?* I wondered. I really felt that I'd gone off the deep end.

But in six months to a year, I realized that I hadn't gone off the deep end. My life was changed. Years later, I was in a debate with the head of the history department at a Midwestern university, and when I said my life had been changed, he interrupted me: "McDowell, are you trying to tell us that God really changed your life? What areas?" After forty-five minutes, he said, "Okay, that's enough."

Mended Relationships

One area I told him about was my restlessness. I always had to be occupied. But a few months after I made that decision for Christ, a kind of mental peace developed. Don't misunderstand—I'm not talking about the absence of conflict. What I found in this relationship with Jesus wasn't as much the absence of conflict as the ability to cope with it. I wouldn't trade that for anything in the world.

Another area that started to change was my bad temper. My temper was such a part of me that I didn't consciously seek to change it. I arrived at the crisis of losing my temper only to find it was gone.

There's another area of which I'm not proud. That area is hatred. I had a lot of hatred in my life. It wasn't something outwardly manifested, but there was a kind of inward grinding. Like so many other people, I was insecure. Every time I met someone different from me, he became a threat to me. I mention it because a lot of people need to have the same change in their lives, and I found the source of change: a relationship with the resurrected, living Christ.

But I hated one man more than anyone else in the world. My father. To me, he was the town alcoholic. If you're from a small town and one of your parents is an alcoholic, you know what I'm talking about. Everybody knows. My friends would come to high school and make jokes about my father being downtown. They didn't think it bothered me. I was like other people, laughing on the outside, but let me tell you, I was crying on the inside. When we had friends over, I would take my father out, tie him up in the barn, and park the car up around the silo. We would tell our friends he'd had to go somewhere.

Maybe five months after I made that decision for Christ, love from God through Jesus Christ entered my life and was so strong it took that hatred and turned it upside down. I was able to look my father squarely in the eye and say, "Dad, I love you." And I really meant it. Given some of the things I'd done, that really shook him up.

After I transferred to a private university, I was in a serious car accident. My neck was in traction. I was taken home, and I'll never forget my father coming into my room. He said, "Son, how can you love a father like me?"

"Dad, I let Christ come into my life. I can't explain it completely, but as a result of that relationship, I've found the capacity to love and accept not only you but other people just the way they are."

Forty-five minutes later, one of the greatest thrills of my life occurred. Somebody in my own family, someone who knew me so well I couldn't pull the wool over his eyes, said to me, "Son, if God can do in my life what I've seen him do in yours, then I want to give him the opportunity." Right there my father prayed with me and trusted Christ.

After I accepted Christ, my life changed within six to eighteen months. My father's life changed right before my eyes. I've never seen such a rapid change. My father touched whiskey only once after that day. He got it as far as his lips, and that was it. I've come to one conclusion: a relationship with Jesus Christ changes lives.

You can laugh at Christianity; you can mock and ridicule it. But it works. If you trust Christ, start watching your attitudes and actions, because Jesus Christ is in the business of changing lives. But Christianity is not something you shove down somebody's throat or force on someone. All I can do is share what I've learned.

If you do decide to follow Jesus, you'll experience what I did—meaning and happiness. And your restlessness, your desire for power and prestige, and your hatred will be replaced with love that surpasses all understanding. It's a relationship that changed my heart, and it changed the people around me as well. It will do the same for you.

25

Dwight L Johnson

Dwight L. Johnson understands that men can't thrive or even survive in isolation. They need fellowship, accountability, and relationship. He is president of Christian Catalysts, a ministry organization that specializes in fundraising, sponsorship, and promotion of events where believers can network with one another.

Dwight has played a significant role in the Fellowship of Christian Athletes, Youth for Christ, YMCA, Rotary, schools of business, hospitals, Christian Executive Officers, Prison Fellowship, and Promise Keepers. His business consulting is done through Sturgeon Systems, where his expertise is in strategic planning, finance, marketing, and sales development.

Dwight has known and advised many leaders in business, education, and politics. Those who shared their humanity and fallibility got Dwight thinking about the need for that kind of transparency in a broader arena, which gave birth to the first volume of The Transparent Leader, *then to this book.*

Starting a New Legacy of Love

My father taught me one of the most valuable lessons a father could ever teach a son. The problem was that he didn't even know he was teaching it to me, nor did he know that if I was going to learn the lesson, I would need to do things a lot differently than he had.

The Family Business

My grandfather started an electrical contracting business in 1911, and he and my father built it up to a level where it had a solid reputation in the Denver area. After I graduated from the University of Colorado, I received a commission in the US Navy through the NROTC, and my wife, Betsy, and I were married. When I got out of the navy in 1962, my dad hired me to go out and bring in customers. I looked forward to this opportunity because I thought it would give me the chance to be close to my dad. When I was in high school in Denver, I was all-city in three sports, but my dad never made it to a single athletic event. He was too busy running the family business. Going to work for him would provide me the link to him that I had missed growing up.

Or so I thought.

Our agreement was that he would be my mentor in the business and spend a minimum of ten hours per week with me, teaching me what he knew. We ended up spending ten hours together in my first six months there—if that. Working in the family business was not what I thought it was going to be.

The first big project I got involved in was when the owner of a large local mortuary bought a mountain above Denver and wanted to build a mausoleum on top of it. He also wanted to build a gigantic cross and hired me to figure out how to do it. I did the calculations, built a model, and got the contract to build the cross. On Easter Sunday 1964, we turned it on. At the time, it was the largest lighted cross in the world. Pilots could see it from more than one hundred miles away. Nearly all of Denver could see it approximately fifty miles away.

It was a project that appeared to set my course as a successful electrical lighting engineer, but even then, Dad couldn't compliment me on the incredible success of the project. He didn't go to New York City with me when I won first place against thirteen other countries in the international competition for the top lighting project in the world.

But the following year, everything changed. The South Platte River flood, one of the worst in Colorado's history, took out a significant part of the state. We had about nine feet of water in our building and about twelve feet in various places around our property. The flood took eighty-three of our trucks and most of our small tool and material inventory. It took several weeks to get things cleaned up enough to move back into our building. Even when we did, though, it seemed like my dad never recovered.

He had worked all his adult life to build this business. In a two-hour span, he lost one-half of his entire net worth.

To try to build the business back up, I cosigned a business loan with my dad. Again I thought it would help our relationship, but it seemed to only make it worse. The more I got involved in how the company worked, the more distant and even hostile he became. It got to a point where if he came in the front door, I headed out the back to avoid any conflict with him.

Most of the board felt that the business should be run a certain way, but the majority owner, Dad, disagreed. It seemed as though every day one of the department heads would approach me and ask, "What are we going to do about your dad?"

To make things even more complicated, our business took a turn for the worse, and we started losing money. Debts piled up. Soon after that, I was in the hospital with a serious ulcer. My mom knew that my condition had a lot to do with my relationship with my dad.

"What are we going to do about this?" she asked.

"I don't know, Mom," I said. "I love my dad, but I am vehemently opposed to my boss. They are the same person."

Hard Decisions

After she left that night, I had what I can describe only as a moment of spiritual renewal. As a young man, I had given my life to Christ through the Fellowship of Christian Athletes up at Estes Park, Colorado, at the first summer conference in 1956, but this experience with my health, the family business, and my dad showed me that I hadn't really given everything to God. That became clear to me in the hospital. I told God that from that moment on, he would be first in my life and could have everything.

After I recovered, I worked out a plan to buy my dad out of the business. I went to some of the vice presidents, and they took second mortgages on their houses and sold other assets, all to be in the position of buying my dad's interest in the company. We knew there was no way the company would go the way we needed it to go if he was still the majority owner or involved at all.

At first he agreed to it, but then the day after Christmas, he said the deal was off. He said he didn't want to go out of the business that early in his life, because this was all he really knew.

All along, I kept meeting with a small group of men for weekly prayer and Bible study. Something I learned during those early days with FCA was that meeting with an accountability and prayer group on a regular basis is one of the keys to continued spiritual health. I told the men that I wondered where God was in this ordeal, and one of them said that God never said things would be easy but that whatever happened would be the right thing. So the group committed this entire transaction to God and asked for his direction and intervention. I had a strange confidence when I told the other executives, "I have the assurance that whatever happens, God is in charge and will direct us."

But two people who should have been involved in this from the beginning had been left out: my wife and my mom. It's never a good idea to have these kinds of negotiations and conflicts without including the most important people in our lives. So finally both my parents had a sit-down meeting with Betsy and me that lasted more than three hours. It was very healthy and open, but my dad was a hard guy to read, and when he and Mom left, I still didn't know what he would do. If he accepted the buyout offer, he was out of the picture. If he didn't, I was unemployed.

Monday morning, my dad walked into the office and said, "Your mother was right last night, and I am sorry. The deal is back on. Let's close it next week."

We bought Dad out, and at our first board meeting, we dedicated the entire company to God. We vowed that we would give all that we possibly could to not-for-profit organizations doing Christian work, and within a few years, we had increased the volume of the company 500 percent.

Our Good Father

At first my dad told many people in town that I had run him out of the business. That was very difficult to hear. But when I think about how the pressures of his job affected him, I don't think he would have lived much longer if he had stayed in it, and I found out later that he felt the same way about the pressure.

After four years of tremendous growth, an electrical contracting company in Michigan contacted me about merging our businesses. We thought this would be the right move to make us more of a national company, so we joined our company with theirs. It was an extremely profitable move for a few years. Then I began feeling uncomfortable with some of their business practices and told them what I was thinking. Very soon after, I felt pressured to no longer be associated with them. Before long, I was no longer part of that company, and I knew a little bit of what my dad probably had felt.

I worked in real estate and consulted with companies that could draw from my experience in the business world, but most important, I kept involved in FCA. When we moved to San Diego, I got involved with a Christian Executive Officers group, where businesspeople in the area could experience the value of having other believers support them through fellowship, Bible study, and prayer. I also started a nonprofit company called Christian Catalysts, and we were very instrumental in bringing one of the early Promise Keepers events to San Diego, along with providing scholarships for more than two hundred men to attend.

I was with my father when he died in a hospice facility in Colorado. I loved him very much, but I never had the sense that I measured up to his standards. I felt that I could never do enough to please him, could never accomplish enough for him to tell me that he was proud of me.

But I have come to a powerful conclusion in reflecting about my dad. As I grew up, as I went to college, as I went into the navy, as I returned as his employee, and as I bought him out of the company, his love for me was conditional. He did the best he could, having come out of the Depression and World War II and having put himself through the Colorado School of Mines. But he didn't know how to love without strings attached. Dad was one of the most disciplined men I have ever known. He had a tremendous work ethic, he was loyal to his family and employees, he always felt strongly about putting more back into the community than he took out, and he always provided well for his family and employees. He truly was a workaholic and expected all of us to be the same.

The good news, though, is that we have a heavenly Father whose love is unconditional. We can't earn it; we can't buy it; we can't even escape it. That's the kind of father I aspire to be, and that is the Father with whom I want to spend eternity. One of the things I learned in all of this is the importance of building the priorities of my professional life, my personal life, and my family life around Jesus Christ. All other things will fail, but Jesus will never fail.

The cross I designed on that rocky mountain is a great symbol. Our lives must be built on the Rock. All other ground is sinking sand.

Changing the Legacy

As I grew older, I realized how important it is to have a good father. So I vowed that I would be a better father to my children than my father was to me. And while it's never completely clear how good of a father a person is, he can measure it a little by the letters his children write or the special calls he gets after they leave home for college, for jobs, or for their new lives with their spouses.

Years ago, Eric wrote me a letter that I wished I could have written to my father:

> *In so many ways I want to be like you, to emulate you, to think, talk, act, perform and just be you. I am so proud of you! I am so lucky to have you and Mom for parents. I think about how Peter's love for Jesus was so firmly grounded that he was called the Rock. That is where our relationship is as well, firmly grounded on the stability of a solid rock, never weakening, never breaking. . . . I look back on the last fifteen years and see the transformation that you've gone through to be where you are today. God literally had to break you—to make you a broken vessel—for Him to build you back into a powerful tool that God can use, just as He did with King David.*

And finally, when he was in his thirties, married to a wonderful woman, with two beautiful children, he gave me perhaps the highest honor a man could experience:

> *Thank you so much for all you have done for me. I am most thankful for what you have instilled in me that has made me who I am today. Thank you for teaching me about our Lord and what having a personal relationship with Jesus really meant. Thank you for being such a consistent, dependable father. Thank you for always being there for me, whether in the pouring rain or a snowstorm, and for sometimes being the only parent at my games or track meets. Thank you for teaching me what being a father truly meant. You were always such a great role model for me, and now, as a young father, I know what I need to do for my kids to let them know how much I love them. Thank you for always letting me pursue my dreams. Thank you for being such a good sounding board for me. Thank you for trusting in God and me in blessing the second most important thing in my life—my Jenny. Thank you for giving and lifting me up to God and allowing Him to help me become the man I am today. If a man is measured by*

how he raised his kids and how they turn out, I think you can be pretty proud of yourself. More than anything, though, I want you to know how proud I am of you!

Dad, thank you for always putting your faith and relationship with Jesus Christ first and foremost in everything in your life. We both know that God does have a perfect plan for each of us, and He won't ever put us into a situation that we can't handle. Thank you so much for breaking out of the mold that was laid before you as to how a father should be. I shake at the thought of where I would be if you had led the same life as Grandpa did. I loved Grandpa and was truly grateful for him in my life, but you can be so proud of how you loved your boys. What a tremendous legacy of love you have started, Dad! It is something you will be known for always.

Could a more significant thing be said by a son to his dad? That he started a legacy of love, despite his own upbringing?

As I reflect on my life and the mistakes I have made both as a husband and as a father, I realize that when we put our faith in our earthly father, we will oftentimes be disappointed, but when we put our faith in our heavenly Father, we will never be disappointed.

NOTES

Chapter 1: Humility

1. Jerry Coffey, "20 of the Most Memorable Muhammad Ali Quotes," Sportscasting, September 20, 2016, https://www.sportscasting.com/muhammad-ali-quotes/.

2. Lance Pugmire, "Underestimating Muhammad Ali Was the Mistake of a Lifetime, George Foreman Says," Los Angeles Times, June 4, 2016, https://www.latimes.com/sports/boxing/la-sp-muhammad-ali-george-foreman-friendship-20160604-snap-story.html.

3. Pugmire.

Chapter 2: True Power and Security

1. C. S. Lewis, *Mere Christianity* (New York: HarperOne, 2001), 121, 124.

2. Václav Havel, *Disturbing the Peace: A Conversation with Karel Hvížd'ala*, trans. Paul Wilson (New York: Vintage Books, 1991), 119.

Chapter 3: Following the Real Leader

1. Lewis Carroll, *Alice's Adventures in Wonderland*, ed. Richard Kelly (Peterborough, ON: Broadview, 2000), 100.
Chapter 5

Chapter 5: Changing Your Course

1. Henry David Thoreau, *Walden: Or, Life in the Woods* (Boston: Houghton, Mifflin, 1899), 15.

2. John D. Rockefeller, quoted in The Speaker's Quote Book, comp. Roy B. Zuck (Grand Rapids: Kregel, 1997), 260.

Notes

Chapter 9: The Character of the Leader

1. Philip Dormer Stanhope, *Letters Written by the Earl of Chesterfield to His Son* (Philadelphia: J. B. Lippincott, 1876), 304.

Chapter 10: The Role of Challenges in Our Lives

1. Woodrow Wilson, When a Man Comes to Himself (n.p.: CreateSpace, 2015), 3, emphasis mine.

Chapter 11: The Role of Challenges in Our Lives

1. Charles Malik, "Welcome," CMUNC (Christian Mission for the United Nations Community) website, accessed March 25, 2021, https://christianmission-un.org/.

Chapter 13: When God Changes a Heart

1. Jim Wallis, "Dangerous Religion: George W. Bush's Theology of Empire," Mississippi Review 32, no. 3 (Fall 2004): 60–72.

2. John Adams, first inaugural address, March 4, 1797.

3. Letter from John Quincy Adams, dated 27 April, 1837, in "Stray Leaves from an Autograph Collection," Historical Magazine, and Notes and Queries Concerning the Antiquities, History and Biography of America, vol. 4 (New York: Charles B. Richardson, 1860), July edition, 194.

4. Michael Burlingame, ed., Lincoln Observed: The Civil War Dispatches of Noah Brooks (Baltimore: Johns Hopkins University Press, 1998), 210.

5. Remarks Recorded for the 'Back-to-God' Program of the American Legion," February 20, 1955, in Public Papers of the Presidents of the United States: Dwight D. Eisenhower: 1955 (Washington, DC: U.S. Government Printing Office, 1960), 274.

Chapter 16: Faith That Overcomes Doubt

1. Paraphrase from Augustine, The Confessions of St. Augustine; The Imitation of Christ, transs. Edward B. Pusey and William Benham (New York: P. F. Collier & Son, 1909), 5. The original quotation reads, "Our heart is restless, until it repose in Thee."